THE INDUSTRIAL REVOLUTION AND WORK IN NINETEENTH-CENTURY EUROPE

REWRITING HISTORIES
Series editor: Jack R. Censer

SOCIETY AND CULTURE IN THE SLAVE SOUTH
Edited by J. William Harris

GENDER AND AMERICAN HISTORY SINCE 1890
Edited by Barbara Melosh

ATLANTIC AMERICAN SOCIETIES
From Columbus through Abolition
Edited by J. R. McNeill and Alan Karras

NAZISM AND GERMAN SOCIETY 1933–1945
Edited by David Crew

DIVERSITY AND UNITY IN EARLY NORTH AMERICA
Edited by P. Morgan

THE INDUSTRIAL REVOLUTION AND WORK IN NINETEENTH-CENTURY EUROPE

Edited by Lenard R. Berlanstein

London and New York

First published 1992
by Routledge
11 New Fetter Lane, London EC4P 4EE

Simultaneously published in the USA and Canada
by Routledge
a division of Routledge, Chapman and Hall Inc.
29 West 35th Street, New York, NY 10001

Reprinted 1997

Phototypeset in 10 on 12 point Palatino by
Intype, London
Printed in Great Britain by
Clays Ltd, St Ives plc

British Library Cataloguing in Publication Data
A CIP catalogue record for this book is available
from the British Library

Library of Congress Cataloguing in Publication Data
The Industrial Revolution and work in nineteenth-century Europe /
edited by Lenard R. Berlanstein
p. cm. — (Rewriting histories)
Includes bibliographical references.
1. Europe—Industries—History—19th century. 2. Europe—
Economic conditions—19th century. 3. Working class—Europe—
History—19th century. I. Berlanstein, Lenard R. II. Series
HC240.I533 1992
305.5'62'0940934—dc 20   91–45629

ISBN 0–415–07052–X ISBN 0–415–07053–8 (pbk)

CONTENTS

CONTENTS

Part III The making of a working class

EDITOR'S PREFACE

Rewriting history, or revisionism, has always followed closely in the tow of history writing. In their efforts to re-evaluate the past, professional as well as amateur scholars have followed many approaches, most commonly as empiricists, uncovering new information to challenge earlier accounts. Historians have also revised previous versions by adopting new perspectives, usually fortified by new research, which overturn received views.

Even though rewriting is constantly taking place, historians' attitudes towards using new interpretations have been anything but settled. For most, the validity of revisionism lies in providing a stronger, more convincing account that better captures the objective truth of the matter. Although such historians might agree that we never finally arrive at the 'truth', they believe it exists and over time may be better and better approximated. At the other extreme stand scholars who believe that each generation or even each cultural group or subgroup necessarily regards the past differently, each creating for itself a more usable history. Although these latter scholars do not reject the possibility of demonstrating empirically that some contentions are better than others, they focus upon generating new views based upon different life experiences. Different truths exist for different groups. Surely such an understanding, by emphasizing subjectivity, further encourages rewriting history. Between these two groups are those historians who wish to borrow from both sides. This third group, while accepting that every congerie of individuals sees matters differently, still wishes somewhat contradictorily to fashion a broader history that incorporates both of these particular visions. Revisionists who stress empiricism fall into the first of the three camps, while others spread out across the board.

Today the rewriting of history seems to have accelerated to a blinding speed as a consequence of the evolution of revisionism. A variety of approaches has emerged. A major factor in this process has been the enormous increase in the number of researchers. This explosion has reinforced and enabled the retesting of many assertions. Significant ideological shifts have also played a major part in the growth of revisionism. First, the crisis of Marxism, culminating in the events in eastern Europe in 1989, has given rise to doubts about explicitly Marxist accounts. Such doubts have spilled over into the entire field of social history which has been a dominant subfield of the discipline for several decades. Focusing on society and its class divisions implies that these are the most important elements in historical analysis. Because Marxism was built on the same claim, the whole basis of social history has been questioned, despite the very many studies that had little directly to do with Marxism. Disillusionment with social history simultaneously opened the door to cultural and linguistic approaches largely developed in anthropology and literature. Multiculturalism and feminism further generated revisionism. By claiming that scholars had, wittingly or not, operated from a white European/American male point of view, newer researchers argued other approaches had been neglected or misunderstood. Not surprisingly, these last historians are the most likely to envision each subgroup rewriting its own usable history, while other scholars incline towards revisionism as part of the search for some stable truth.

Rewriting Histories will make these new approaches available to the student population. Often new scholarly debates take place in the scattered issues of journals which are sometimes difficult to find. Furthermore, in these first interactions, historians tend to address one another, leaving out the evidence that would make their arguments more accessible to the uninitiated. This series of books will collect in one place a strong group of the major articles in selected fields, adding notes and introductions conducive to improved understanding. Editors will select articles containing substantial historical data, so that students – at the least those who approach the subject as an objective phenomenon – can advance, not only their comprehension of debated points, but also their grasp of substantive aspects of the subject.

Labour history, as Berlanstein's volume illustrates, has been the subject of significant revisionism. For many years scholars focused on 'the Industrial Revolution' as the pre-eminent moment of economic growth and technological change, sweeping away older forms of work and massively altering wage-earners' lives. A careful consideration of workers came only with the development of 'history from below' since the 1960s. The more historians examined economic development from the labourers' point of view and from cultural perspectives, the more they have realized the need to rethink the Industrial Revolution.

Jack R. Censer

GENERAL INTRODUCTION

The Industrial Revolution is central to our understanding of the modern world. One distinguished scholar, Harold Perkin, describes it as 'a revolution in men's access to the means of life, in control over their ecological environment, in their capacity to escape from the tyranny and niggardliness of nature'.[1] Another ranks the Industrial Revolution with the advent of monotheism and the development of language as a fundamental break in human affairs.[2] Virtually every western civilization textbook devotes a chapter to the Industrial Revolution, usually following one on the French Revolution. An introduction customarily announces that the two revolutions laid the foundations for contemporary life, one delineating the political trajectory and the other marking the socio-economic path the west would follow in the subsequent 200 years.

The textbook chapter on the Industrial Revolution always begins with a survey of the legendary inventions which engendered factory production in the late eighteenth century: the spinning jenny, the flying shuttle, the Cort puddling and rolling process in ironmaking and so on. The geographical focus is on Lancashire, England, home to the infamous 'dark, satanic mills' in which cotton fabric was produced. These mills undercut hand-spinning (and eventually weaving) and marked mechanized, factory production as the wave of the future. Descriptions of the Industrial Revolution inevitably note the ambiguous tone struck by all early witnesses, who were both excited and frightened by what they saw. On the one hand, there was no doubt that wealth was being created for some on an unprecedented scale. On the other hand, the concentration of impoverished workers in pestilent cities shocked

Englishmen and made many continental Europeans thankful that their homeland lagged behind in this development. Textbooks duly record the immediate high cost of the Industrial Revolution in terms of soaring mortality rates, declining literacy rates, vicious work accidents and (since children as young as 6 worked in the mills) lost childhoods.

About the long-term consequences, historians are generally far more optimistic. They cite the creation of millions of new jobs for a rising population which needed them, the gradual improvements in the standard of living for the masses and the emergence of a prosperous, self-confident middle class. Though the term 'revolution' implies a sudden change, authors invariably insist that these alterations took years to materialize. The Industrial Revolution was largely a British phenomenon during the first half of the nineteenth century; the Continent required the rest of the century, at least, to approach Britain's achievements.

The Industrial Revolution fixes the historian's gaze on factories, on cities, on sophisticated technology, on the trend towards bigness, on the emerging factory proletariat and on the harsh discipline at the shop-floor. Is there anything amiss in this conventional portrait? Is this not what the making of the modern world was all about?

The historian's critical task involves more than accumulating facts and building them into generalizations. Scholars must also take care that interpretations do not assume a life of their own, channelling analysis in a particular direction. For better or worse, a perfect impartiality and a heroic openness to all options do not characterize even the most fastidious investigations of a subject. Research generally occurs within established paradigms, or general explanatory frameworks, whose assumptions and limits are rarely examined. Paradigms define the problems which are open to scrutiny – and those which are not – for a scholarly community. Could it be that the Industrial Revolution is so widely accepted, not so much because it is a self-evident fact, but because it has been the reigning paradigm for discussing socio-economic change in the modern era? The central question posed by this volume is whether the Industrial Revolution is not one of those conceptualizations which narrows and misleads as much as it informs. As a first approach to treating the questions, it is worth noting that the concept of an industrial revolution did not appear spontaneously with factory development in the late eighteenth and early nineteenth centuries. It was the invention of an identifiable scholar at a particular moment. We may trace the idea back to Arnold Toynbee's *Lectures on the Industrial Revolution in England*, published in 1884. The notion enjoyed immediate acceptance; but was this because Toynbee had hit on the truth? That the concept took root at a moment of intense international economic competition, a faltering of British industrial supremacy and expanding imperialism suggests that the answer might well be more complex.

In fact, much of the historical scholarship of the last three decades rests uneasily within the paradigm of industrial revolution. The scholarship, variously known as 'history from below', 'the new labour history' or just 'social history', has focused attention on the actual experience of the labourers during the era of the Industrial Revolution. Since the 1960s, historians have shown a greater willingness to question the benefits of economic development for the masses and, to a degree, have placed more emphasis on matters of social justice than on growth. By doing so, the new historical trends reopened issues that had once been treated as settled and posed new questions that proved to be important and revealing. What sort of work did most wage-earners actually do? How central were the factory and sophisticated technology to their work? Did male and female workers experience change in the same way? Were the growth of population and of cities inevitably tied to the emergence of an industrial order? Was the work routine in the 'dark, satanic mills' so very different from earlier situations? The new labour history has not always arrived at answers that accord well with the model of a dramatic industrial revolution convulsing all in its path.

Intensive investigation of society before, during and after the Industrial Revolution has undermined the view that events in Britain between 1760 and 1840 were decisive to the emergence of the modern world. Textbooks (and even more advanced works) usually support such a perspective by conflating the Industrial Revolution with other great socioeconomic transformations. However, social historians have made a good case for each revolution being distinct. Given that the European population grew from roughly 150 million in 1750 to 260 million in 1850, it has been conventional to treat the Industrial and the Demographic Revolutions as part of the same process. Yet few experts today would deny that the two might well have had different sources and different consequences.[3] Similarly, the link between urban growth and industrialization was not at all as strong on the Continent as it was for Britain. On the whole, historians are much more reluctant to posit one single model for socio-economic change or to look to nineteenth-century Britain for that model.

New labour historians of the last three decades have paid special attention to the work experience on the shop-floor and have come to question received wisdom about the special nature of the factory. David Landes, who wrote a landmark book in the field before the new research became widely known, asserted that factory discipline represented a decisive break with earlier work situations. In his view, the wage-earner was 'broken to the inexorable demands of the clock'.[4] What we now know does not allow for such sharp distinctions between the traditional workshop and the emerging factory.

Conventions in the writing of nineteenth-century political history have also reinforced the apocalyptic view of the Industrial Revolution, perhaps at the cost of accuracy. When grappling with the great upheavals in political life – the birth of vast labour movement, working-class rebellions, revolutions and the growth of strong socialist parties – it was standard practice to associate the changes with industrialization. Consciously or not, historians accepted the link that Karl Marx made. His ideology identified the factory proletariat as the agents of revolution and dismissed older sorts of wage-earners as irrelevant because destined to disappear with economic development. The power of paradigms to shape research is quite apparent in the way factory workers were taken as the prototype of the nineteenth-century worker even though all available statistics showed they were a minority, and a rather small one at that.

Labour historians have had to break out of the constraints of the Industrial Revolution model in order to come to grips with nineteenth-century class conflict. It turns out that factory proletarians were marginal to class action. Just the workers whom Marx wrote off – craftsmen and other traditional labourers – created the working-class movements and gave them mass support. Here is another way in which the Industrial Revolution looms less large in our current thinking about social history.

The Industrial Revolution is not a self-evident fact which helps us to know the past. It is a mental construct with inherent presuppositions and limits. An economic historian's recent attempt to encapsulate its significance reveals much about the intellectual baggage that underpins the concept. He asserts that 'Britain taught Europe and Europe taught the world how the miracles of technology and efficient management can break the shackles of poverty and want.'[5] The claim presupposes linear, unidirectional, unproblematic progression towards universal abundance. It is based on a glowing appreciation of material progress and a confidence in its inevitability. The assertion contains some truth, but it would be foolish to overlook the distortions. After all, 200 years after the Industrial Revolution supposedly began, more than half of humanity is still oppressed by the shackles of poverty and want. Furthermore, the technological and managerial advances achieved in industrializing Britain have not always been applied to creating global prosperity. Very often they were the sources of oppression, reduced prosperity and lost opportunities. To accept the notion of an industrial revolution that forever changed the world is, at best, to construct a partial view of the past.

Should professors, then, think seriously about tearing up their lectures on the Industrial Revolution and ripping out the chapter from the textbooks? If we dare to punch holes in, or even disregard, the paradigm, what remains? Are there alternatives? The contributors to this volume have some intriguing answers. The general thrust of the essays by David Cannadine, Charles Tilly and Raphael Samuel is to replace the notion of the Industrial Revolution with a process of social transformation that was older, broader, more diffuse and more multidirectional. Theresa McBride, Christopher Johnson and James Roberts reinforce such rethinking with their studies of workers' experiences on the job. They show that a focus on the iron discipline in factories does not do justice to the diversity or even pinpoint the sources of labourers' discontents. A third section of readings addresses questions of class consciousness and worker protest. These essays underscore the continuous nature of scholarly revisionism in that William Sewell and Joan Scott take the dismissal of the Industrial Revolution as given and focus a critical eye on the new social history. These authors argue that we will never understand workers' movements without adopting iconoclastic approaches to politics and culture. Their work takes us to the current cutting edge of historical research.

One might reasonably claim that critics have not left the Industrial Revolution entirely bereft of meaning. None the less, impressive advances in our understanding of the past have come from ignoring the concept. The new approaches will inevitably yield their own orthodoxies – some scholars insist they already have. These orthodoxies will be questioned in turn. There is always a future in history!

NOTES

1 Harold Perkins, *Origins of Modern English Society* (London, 1969): 3.
2 Joel Mokyr, 'The Industrial Revolution and the new economic history', in Joel Mokyr (ed.), *The Economics of the Industrial Revolution* (Totowa, NJ, 1985): 2.
3 See Michael Flynn, *The European Demographic System, 1500–1820* (Baltimore, Maryland, 1981).
4 David S. Landes, *The Unbound Prometheus. Technological Change and Industrial Development in Western Europe from 1750 to the Present* (Cambridge, 1969): 2.
5 Mokyr, 'Industrial Revolution': 44.

Part I

RETHINKING THE INDUSTRIAL REVOLUTION

The notion of the Industrial Revolution has been used for a century and is well established in textbooks. Why bother to displace it? In fact, as David Cannadine shows, studies of the Industrial Revolution have continually reinvented its essence. Moreover, Raphael Samuel raises the possibility that it is simply not accurate as a description of socio-economic change. Charles Tilly undertakes the daunting task of providing an alternate way of thinking about the vast forces which have forged a new social order over the past two and a half centuries. The reader will have to judge whether breaking with a classic notion of the Industrial Revolution creates intellectual chaos or provides a deeper understanding of the past.

1

THE PRESENT AND THE PAST IN THE ENGLISH INDUSTRIAL REVOLUTION, 1880–1980

David Cannadine

Studying the evolution of historical thought on a subject often dispels the scientific pretensions of the discipline. It quickly becomes apparent that historians' ideas are very much bound by time and place. Letting the facts speak for themselves is not in the order of things. David Cannadine offers a stunning demonstration of this point regarding the Industrial Revolution. He shows that scholars, over time, have stressed very different aspects of it and that the differing interpretations are closely tied to the dominant economic conditions of the era.

Students should note two limitations which the author places on the analysis. He is concerned exclusively with the writings of economic historians and with the English Industrial Revolution, long taken as the classic case. It would be interesting to learn if the conclusions would be different had Cannadine considered the Continent and other sorts of scholars. There is room to doubt that it would.

In addition to making the reader sensitive to the relativity of historical analysis, Cannadine's essay also makes us aware of recurrent themes. It might not be outlandish to conclude that interpretations of the Industrial Revolution are locked in a cycle: concern for the poor giving way to concern for economic growth at all costs. Readers can make this essay relevant to all those that follow by asking how much is brand new and how much is a reversion to a former interpretative trend. If an argument does recur, is it for the same reason that produced the original? Cannadine would always insist that there is a lot of the present in what we say about the past.

* * *

This article suggests four phases into which economic history writing may be divided during the hundred years since Toynbee's *Lectures on the Industrial Revolution* effectively began modern discussion of the subject.[1] The first section explores the years to the 1920s, when contemporary preoccupations with social surveys and poverty influenced the prevailing interpretation of the Industrial Revolution, which emphasized its disagreeable human consequences. By contrast, the second generation of economic historians, writing from the mid-1920s to the early 1950s, reflected current concerns with war and economic fluctuations by stressing the cyclical nature of the industrialization process. Their successors, who wrote from the mid-1950s to the early 1970s, were influenced by the rise of development economics and by the post-war efflorescence of western capitalism and so rewrote the Industrial Revolution once more, this time as the first instance of 'economic growth'. Finally, since 1974, as economic growth has become simultaneously less attractive and less attainable, the Industrial Revolution has been given another new identity, this time as something less spectacular and more evolutionary than was previously supposed. Such is the outline of economic history writing on the Industrial Revolution to be advanced here. And, in the light of it, a more speculative attempt will then be made to explore the mechanism by which this process of generational change and interpretational evolution actually operates.

I

The years from the 1880s to the early 1920s were the first period in which self-conscious economic historians investigated the Industrial Revolution, and they did so against a complex background of hopes and fears about the society and economy of the time, which greatly influenced the perspective they took on it. Neo-classical economists like Marshall[a] were moderately buoyant about the economy during this period: but for politicians, businessmen and landowners, the prospects seemed less bright.[2] Prices were falling, profits were correspondingly reduced and foreign competition was growing: faith in unlimited economic progress was greatly diminished.[3] Royal commissions investigated depressions in industry, trade and agriculture; the Boer War[b] revealed a nation whose military were incompetent and whose manhood was unfit; and tariff reform was partly based on a recognition that there were, in the economy, unmistakable signs of decay.[4] At the same time, the working class was increasingly enfranchised, there was a growing belief that government must be more actively interventionist on their behalf, trade-unionist membership went up remarkably and there were explosions of industrial unrest in the 1880s and early 1910s.

More particularly, from the 1880s, there was a major revival of interest in the 'condition of England' question, particularly with regard to health, housing and poverty. The reasons for this 'remarkable flowering in the social concern of the English middle classes' in that decade, and the extent to which it did (or did not) represent a new departure in social and sociological thought, remain sources of academic controversy.[5] But what is *not* in dispute is the massive outpouring of best-selling literature on the subject in the thirty years before the First World War, including the *Royal Commission on the Housing of the Working Class*, the surveys by Booth and Rowntree,[c] the investigative journalism sparked off by Mearns's *Bitter Cry*, the evocations of slum life in novels such as Morrison's *Child of the Jago* and the writings of members of the Liberal intelligentsia such as C. F. G. Masterman.[6] Together, this great outpouring constituted a guilt-ridden, fearful recognition that poverty and squalor were not the product of individual shortcomings, but were endemic in a system which created so much want in the midst of so much plenty. It was, as Henry George put it memorably, 'this association of poverty with progress' which was 'the great enigma of our times'.[7] 'What' enquired Asquith, reformulating the same proposition more broadly:

> is the use of talking about Empire if here, at its very centre, there is always to be found a mass of people, stunted in education, a prey of intemperance, huddled and congested beyond the possibility of realizing in any true sense either social or domestic life?[8]

Such contemporary revelations exerted a powerful influence, diverting scholarly attention towards what G. N. Clark felicitously described as 'social concern with economic conditions'.[9] For the majority of people, it seemed, the Industrial Revolution *had not worked*, and it was the desire to discover what had

5

gone wrong which prompted many of the pioneering studies of the economy of late eighteenth- and early nineteenth-century England. Indeed, it was Toynbee himself who stated most explicitly this close link between the present and the past in the history of the Industrial Revolution. 'It would be well', he argued:

> if in studying the past we could always bear in mind the problems of the present. . . . You must have some principle of selection, and you could not have a better one than to pay special attention to the history of the social problems which are agitating the world now, for you may be sure that they are problems not of temporary but of lasting importance.[10]

Toynbee, as Milner later explained, 'was on fire with the idea of a great improvement' in the material condition of the working classes, and precisely exemplified that upper-middle-class sense of guilt which Beatrice Webb was later to describe.[11] Indeed, in *My Apprenticeship* she quoted with approval Toynbee's most anguished and contrite words:

> We – the middle classes, I mean, not merely the very rich – we have neglected you; instead of justice we have offered you charity; and instead of sympathy we have offered you hard and unreal advice; but I think we are changing. . . . We have wronged you; we have sinned against you grievously . . . ; but if you will forgive us . . . we will serve you, we will devote our lives to your service.[12]

This desire to locate the historical origins of unacceptable contemporary social conditions in the Industrial Revolution was equally strong in the Hammonds and Webbs. As P. F. Clarke explains, the Hammonds did make 'an effort at objectivity which gave their work its scholarly value'; but at the same time they were also 'deeply committed political figures'. *The Village Labourer*, for instance, was described by the Longmans reader as 'sound historically, though written from a radical point of view', and by Gilbert Murray as showing 'how blind the whole upper and middle class can be to the condition of the poor' – a phrase which had particularly strong resonances given the prevailing concerns of the time. Indeed, as an anti-

6

landlord polemic, the book provided an historical preface to Lloyd George's land campaign,[d] with its argument that, between 1760 and 1830, the outcome might have been different in the countryside if only the upper classes had been more responsible. Likewise, its sequel, *The Town Labourer*, was anti-capital and anti-*laissez-faire*, 'destroying', as Tawney explained, 'the historical assumptions on which our modern slavery is based'.[13] Above all, the Hammonds' books provided, in their portraits of rapacious landlords and conscienceless capitalists, historical support for the view that free enterprise must be controlled, that the state must be more interventionist and that trade unions should be protected and strengthened.

The Webbs' writings on the Industrial Revolution contained a similar prescriptive thrust. Beatrice was profoundly influenced by her early work for Booth, was racked with guilt about the sufferings of the lower classes and saw explicit links between the bad conditions of the present and the horrors of the Industrial Revolution:

> A study of British blue books, illuminated by my own investigations into the chronic poverty of our great cities, opened my eyes to the workers' side of the picture. To the working class of Great Britain in the latter half of the eighteenth and first half of the nineteenth century – that is four-fifths of the entire population – the 'Industrial Revolution' . . . must have appeared . . . as a gigantic and cruel experiment which, insofar as it was affecting their homes, their health, their subsistence and their pleasure, was proving a calamitous failure.[14]

For Beatrice, as for Sidney, the past record and present circumstances both showed that what was needed was 'collective regulation of the conditions of employment . . . by legislative enactment or by collective bargaining':[15] in short, an end to *laissez-faire*, by promoting stronger unions and greater state intervention. For the Webbs as for the Hammonds, their writings about the Industrial Revolution were essentially historical prefaces to contemporary problems. As Beatrice explained, their *History of Trade Unions* was 'little more than a historical introduction to the task we had set before us: the scientific analysis of the structure and function of British trade unions', and their *History of Local Government* was but the prologue to 'an analysis of English local government as it existed in our own time for the use of would-be reformers'.[16]

Thus influenced and motivated, Toynbee, the Hammonds and the Webbs established the dominant interpretation of the Industrial Revolution in their generation as 'the history of the social problems which are agitating the world now'. It was rapid; it was terrible; and it was so primarily because of a lack of humane government intervention. For Toynbee, the old o.der 'was suddenly broken in pieces by the mighty blows of the steam engine and the powerloom'; innovations 'destroyed the old world and built a new one'; it was a period of 'economic revolution and anarchy'.[17] For the Webbs, the Industrial Revolution was characterized by 'wholesale adoption of power-driven machinery and the factory system', which 'took place around 1780'.[18] And for the Hammonds it 'separated England from her past as completely as the political revolution separated France from her past'; the 'history of the early years of the Industrial Revolution' was 'a history of vast and rapid expansion'; it was 'a departure in which man passed definitely from one world to another'.[19]

What made this especially dreadful were the 'evils of unrestricted and unregulated capitalism'.[20] *Laissez-faire*, the new ideology of the ruling and capitalist classes, which denied to the labourer the fruits of his work and condemned him to a life of poverty and squalor, was assailed with sustained and impassioned disapproval. For Toynbee, 'complete and unhesitating trust in individual self-interest' was the same as 'the weak being trampled under foot'. 'This kind of competition', he concluded, 'has to be checked.'[21] In *The Town Labourer*, the Hammonds devoted two chapters to the minds of the ruling class, condemning them as the 'generation that left the workmen to their fate in the Industrial Revolution', who were 'powerless and helpless, needing the protection of the law and parliament' which, of course, they did not obtain.[22] And the Webbs, too, saw *laissez-faire*, 'fully established in Parliament as an authoritative industrial doctrine of political economy', as leading to squalid conditions in industrial towns and to the suppression of trade unions. 'With free competition', they concluded, 'and private property in land and capital, no individual can possibly obtain the full fruits of his own labour'.[23]

Set against this background of so all-pervasive a view,

Clapham's riposte in the first volume of his *Economic History of Modern Britain* seems even more pointed than is usually allowed, challenging all three facets of the Industrial Revolution which most earlier writers had stressed. In the first place, he offered a different picture of its timing from that which had prevailed since Toynbee. He showed how gradual and localized the Industrial Revolution was, stressed 'the diversity of the national economic life', examined in great detail the predominant and non-mechanized industries and noted how little change there had been by 1851. His book was, in Herbert Heaton's phrase, a 'study in slow motion', which repeatedly insisted that 'no single British industry had passed through a complete technological revolution before 1830'. 'The Lancashire cotton operative', Clapham noted, 'was not the representative workman of the Britain of King George IV';[e] 'the man of the crowded countryside was still the typical Englishman'; 'the steam engine itself . . . was still small and, outside a limited group of leading industries, comparatively little used'.[24]

More explicitly, Clapham attacked 'the legend that everything was getting worse for the working man', by presenting statistics which showed, on the contrary, that in the period after 1790, 'for every class of urban or industrial labourer about which information is available except – a grave exception – such dying trades as common hand loom cotton weaving, wages had risen markedly during the intervening sixty years'.[25] Finally, he examined the record of the government and the legislature, not in the light of criticisms retrospectively levelled, but by the more realistic criterion of what the alternatives were at the time:

> Judged as governments are perhaps entitled to be judged, not by what proved practicable in a later and more experienced day, not by what reformers and poets dreamed and were not called upon to accomplish, but by the achievement of other governments in their own day, that of Britain . . . makes a creditable showing.[26]

II

The period from the mid-1920s to the early 1950s marks the second distinctive phase in the historiography of the Industrial

Revolution. Like the era before, it was characterized by pessimism about the economy and the future of capitalism, but this time it was global rather than merely national. For the international system which had worked relatively smoothly in the halcyon days of the Gold Standard[f] had collapsed beyond recovery after the First World War. In 1923, the Webbs had published *The Decay of Capitalist Civilisation*, which argued that, from 1850, 'it has been receding from defeat to defeat'.[27] But, as M. M. Postan pointed out a decade later, the 'ossification of the system' was so widespread that such pessimism was no longer the monopoly of the left:

> Among the many things which have affected the position of socialists in the post-war world has been the loss of their exclusive rights in 'the decline of capitalism'. . . . However much they differ about the origin and the causation, they all agree about the reality of the disease and its symptoms. The dwindling of international trade, the cessation of international migrations, the strangulation of international credit, recur in official speeches and in letters to the press.[28]

Predictably, the main work of professional economists in these years was concerned with these cyclical fluctuations. For economists with a historical interest, there was an obvious appeal in seeing whether these contemporary cycles could be traced back as far as the Industrial Revolution itself. And for the historian familiar with economic theory, there was an equally strong temptation to apply it directly to the period of the Industrial Revolution to see what might emerge if it was viewed from a cyclical perspective. Either way, these approaches served to establish new interpretations of the Industrial Revolution itself, which were neither indebted to, nor derived from, the earlier interpretational mould. More specifically, the obvious parallels between the wars of 1793–1815 and 1914–18, and the phases of readjustment and depression which followed in both cases, served to focus attention more sharply still on the period from the 1790s to the 1820s. At a time when the Gold Standard had broken down in the twentieth century, there was an obvious temptation to look at the last period, almost exactly 100 years ago, when money, currency, banking and finance had been in so confused and unstable a state. As T. E. Gregory explained, 'the economic and, in particular, the monetary problems which we are facing today have a startling resemblance to those which were the subject matter of contention for two generations a century ago'.[29]

III

Between the mid–1950s and the early 1970s, the unexpected, unprecedented efflorescence of western capitalism combined with limited inflation and full employment to create a rapidly rising standard of living for the majority of the people of western Europe. Of course, rates of growth differed, both between the United States and Europe and within Europe itself: but all western nations benefited, and Britain was no exception. As Postan put it, surveying Europe's post-war development in words much more optimistic than he had used earlier:

> To the historian as well as to the ordinary observer, the unique feature of the post-war economy in the west is its growth. It reveals itself in various signs of ever-mounting affluence, as well as in more sophisticated statistical and economic measurements.[30]

Or, as David S. Landes noted more pithily, 'the European economies seemed to have learned the secret of eternal growth and prosperity'.[31]

For economists and government officials, there were three major consequences of these changes: the decline of interest in the trade cycle, the pursuit of economic growth at home and the rise of development economics. In the two decades from the early 1950s, the business cycle, tamed by Keynesian government policies, assumed so attenuated a form, with growth continuing even in downswings, that one group of economists returned a qualified but definite 'yes' to the question: is the business cycle obsolete?[32] 'Had the idea of the business cycle not existed', observed Martin Gilbert, 'it would hardly have been invented to describe the post-war fluctuations in Europe'.[33] 'The European economy', agreed Postan, 'was all but depression free. Such unevenness and recessions as there were differed from the pre-war ones not only in

11

amplitude but also in timing and significance'.[34] To the more optimistic commentators, indeed, emancipation from the thraldom of cyclical fluctuations seemed complete. 'There is no reason to suppose', wrote Andrew Schonfield, 'that the patterns of the past, which have been ingeniously unravelled by the historians of trade cycles, will reassert themselves in the future'.[35]

So, as the cyclical model was dethroned, the growth model was put in its place.[36] Going for growth became the consuming obsession of western governments, the shared aim of ostensibly opposed political parties and a major preoccupation of applied economists who, extending Keynes's work on investment,[g] assigned to capital a crucial role in the growth process.[37] 'In all European countries', Postan remarked, 'economic growth became a universal creed, and a common expectation to which governments were expected to conform. To that extent, economic growth was the product of economic growthmanship'.[38] Nations within Europe aspired to outdo each other in growth, and all sought to catch up the United States. In so far as government planning agencies were introduced, it was to plan for growth, as in France between 1948–65, and as in Britain with the settling up of NEDC in 1962.[h] Significantly, the Labour government's National Plan, introduced in 1965, was described as 'a plan to provide the basis for greater economic growth'. As Sir Roy Harrod put it two years later, 'growth . . . has priority over all other objectives'.[39]

One consequence of the west's buoyancy about its own prosperity and its capacity to engineer and manage that prosperity was the growing belief that it might be possible to accomplish similar economic miracles of development in the Third World, via technical assistance, trade and (especially) the injection of capital. As Kennedy proclaimed in his inaugural speech, in the high noon of western optimism: 'To those people in the huts and villages of half the globe struggling to break the bonds of mass misery, we pledge our best efforts to help them help themselves.' In practice, this meant a massive expansion in foreign aid, to be deployed according to the prescriptions laid down by development economists, who were the burgeoning first cousins of growth economists.[40] The success of the Marshall Plan[i] in reviving war-weary Europe seemed to augur well for parallel endeavours further afield; the affinity between the problems of unemployment in the west and underemployment in the Third World seemed clear; and it was but a short step from investment for growth at home to investment for development abroad. On both fronts, it was the commitment to growth, and the belief that this could be brought about by 'a massive injection of capital', which was of crucial significance.[41]

All this profoundly influenced the way in which economic historians addressed the Industrial Revolution. Rostow, for example, in the 1950s, shifted his interests from fluctuations to growth. In the first edition of his book with that title, he noted how 'the issues of economic development from relatively primitive beginnings have increasingly occupied the minds of economists and policy makers in the west'.[42] And within seven years, he reported 'a most remarkable surge of thought centred on the process of economic growth'. 'A good part', he added, 'of the contemporary effort in economic history is directly shaped by the concern with public policy designed to accelerate growth in the underdeveloped regions of the world, which emerged in the decade after World War Two'.[43] So, the Industrial Revolution was no longer seen as something terrible because unregulated, or cyclical because unregulated, but as the first example of sustained economic growth which accomplished in England by private enterprise what must now be promoted in the Third World by government agency. It ceased to seem something *bad* which should have been *tamed* by government intervention, and became instead something *good* which must be *replicated* by government aid.

Accordingly, as Rostow further observed, 'the major common task and meeting place of economists and historians are to be found in the analysis of economic growth';[44] and, in his best-selling book, *The Stages of Economic Growth*, he offered his own contribution, as an economic historian, 'to the formation of a wiser public policy'. It was, explicitly, 'a non-communist manifesto', which argued how and why the west could bring economic development to the Third World more efficiently and satisfactorily than Soviet Russia.[45] It was addressed, not only to policy-makers at home, but to 'the men in Djakarta, Rangoon, New Delhi and Karachi; the men in Tehran, Baghdad, and Cairo; the men south of the desert too, in Accra, Lagos, and Salisbury'. And its message was simple: that the study of industrial revolutions in the past offered the best guide to the promotion of economic development in the future. 'It is useful, as well as roughly accurate', he noted, 'to regard the process of development now going forward in Asia, the Middle East, Africa, and Latin America as analogous to the stages of preconditions and take-off of other societies, in the late eighteenth, nineteenth, and early twentieth centuries'.[46]

More precisely, the study of particular aspects of the growth process was illuminated by these present-day concerns. Hartwell, for instance, felt encouraged to take an 'optimistic' view of the standard of living in the Industrial Revolution because there was *a priori* scepticism, on the basis of the modern theory of economic development, that economic progress over a long period could make the rich richer and the poor poorer'.[47] Schumpeter's entrepreneur,[j] previously the man who initiated cycles, was given a face-lift, and reappeared as the heroic figure who initiated economic growth. 'The distinctive feature of growth is entrepreneurship', observed Arthur Lewis, and the economic historians nodded their approval.[48] Studies of the rich, the successful and the famous among businessmen mounted, and their sensitivity to economic opportunity, and their part in creating it, was greatly extolled.[49] In the same way, there was a great interest in the part played by banking in financing this first example of economic growth. One such study of finance in the Industrial Revolution was explicitly intended 'to shed light on a pressing practical problem – namely financing economic development' by providing 'development economists, planners and policy makers who are wrestling with the theoretical and practical problems of an industrial take-off with empirical grist for their respective mills'.[50]

Thus was growth established as the predominant interpretation, as the facts of the Industrial Revolution were selected and organized in accordance with the theory of economic development. And yet, even as this happened, there was a recognition among those who employed it that the theory was not entirely appropriate, that the model did not fit completely, that Britain was first to industrialize and therefore more unique than paradigmatic. In part, this arose from the rapid rejection of the more specific parts of Rostow's take-off, as detailed studies of capital accumulation and the role of cotton suggested

14

evolutionary rather than revolutionary progress.[51] More generally, Deane conceded that there was little to be gained from
analysing pre-industrial England as if it was like a contemporary underdeveloped country: it was not over-populated, it was
not 90 per cent agricultural, it was a society rich in resources,
high in literacy and with a well-developed market system.[52]
By 1851, as Mathias, Deane and Landes all admitted, the overall picture of the country and economy was very different
from that suggested by a look at the most advanced sectors:
agriculture was still (if diminishingly) dominant, and the textile
and metal industries employed a relatively small proportion of
the labour force.[53] Indeed, Hartwell went even further, not
only suggesting that the facts of British industrialization in
many ways did not accord to the theories of growth, but also
that, if they showed anything, it was that 'any simple theory
of, or policy for, growth is absurd'.[54]

Such general warnings against the dominance of the
'growth' approach to the Industrial Revolution in the 1960s
were no more widely heeded than were the results of such
detailed researches as also pointed to the same conclusion.
For even if the authors of textbooks were careful to build in
reservations, they still approached the Industrial Revolution
from the standpoint of development economics, hoped that
their findings might be of use to those planning growth in the
Third World and (albeit unintentionally) left many generations
of undergraduates with the sense that it was sudden, successful and largely connected with investment. As long as 'the
problems of the present' remained those of growth at home
and development abroad, this unprecedentedly optimistic picture of the Industrial Revolution, so very different from that
given in the two preceding generations, prevailed. Only when
contemporary circumstances altered again would the reservations made in the growth generation, which themselves
harked back to Clapham's earlier work, become enthroned in
their own right, and in their entirety, as the new interpretation.

IV

Since the mid-1970s, the economic climate has again altered
profoundly. The two decades of unprecedented post-war prosperity came to an abrupt end with the energy crisis of 1973–4,

and were followed by a new menace, stagflation, to which Keynesian economics appeared to offer no antidote. And, at the very time when the certainty of growth was undermined, the appropriateness of it was also brought into question. One view, the environmental, most famously articulated by Schumacher, said that growth *should* not happen: 'one of the most fateful errors of our age', he wrote, in an explicit attack on Galbraith, 'is the belief that "the problem of production" has been solved'.[55] And the other, the ecological, as exemplified by the Club of Rome report, argued that, in any case, continued economic growth *could* not happen because the world's resources would give out: 'for the first time, it has become vital to inquire into the cost of unrestricted material growth, and to consider the alternatives to its continuation'.[56] As Rostow aptly summarized it: 'suddenly, in the 1970's, the inevitability, even the legitimacy, of economic growth was questioned'.[57]

The result was a return of pre-growth economics gloom. 'The most remarkable two decades of economic growth in modern history', Rostow explained, had been superseded by 'the greatest challenge to industrial civilisation since it began to take shape two centuries ago.'[58] Once again his interest has shifted in consequence, from writing historically-grounded development manifestos to evolving 'specific lines of policy which might permit the world community to transit with reasonable success the next quarter century'. For him as for others, the change in circumstances has been remarkable:

> An important turning point occurred in the world econ-
> omy and, indeed, in industrial civilisation during the first
> half of the 1970's. A pattern of economic and social pro-
> gress which had persisted for almost a quarter century
> was broken. Politicians, economists and citizens found
> themselves in a somewhat new and uncomfortable world.
> Familiar modes of thought and action were challenged
> as they no longer seemed to grip the course of events.
> Expectations of the future became uncertain.[59]

Within this generally pessimistic world climate, the British economy has suffered more than most in western Europe. 'No subject', noted Galbraith, 'is so lovingly discussed in our own time as the economic problems of Britain'.[60] 'The British deceleration of the late 1960s', agreed Rostow, 'is more marked than for most of the other major industrial economies, and the subsequent impact of the price revolution of 1972–7 more acute'.[61] Just as Britain shared in the prosperity of the post-war years to a lesser extent than many western countries, so, since 1974, it has fared worse in this renewed age of uncertainty, with higher rates of inflation and greater unemployment.[62] For the pessimists, this has meant regret at the coming of a post-industrialized world, with a broken and fragmented working class, weakened unions, and a divided labour movement.

Instead of being presented as the paradigmatic case, the first and most famous instance of economic growth, the British Industrial Revolution is now depicted in a more negative light, as a limited, restricted, piecemeal phenomenon, in which various things did *not* happen or where, if they did, they had far less effect than was previously supposed. The study of entrepreneurship, for example, has shifted dramatically from the big and the successful to the small and the failed. 'The names that have become famous', P. L. Payne notes, 'were not typical entrepreneurs.' On the contrary, he suggests that the average businessman was more likely to be small-scale and inept than large-scale and successful, a view endorsed by Sheila Marriner, who argues that bankruptcy may have been as typical a condition for entrepreneurs in the classical age of the Industrial Revolution as profits.[63] Even more tellingly, Gatrell and Chapman have explicitly applied the 'limits to growth' view by asking why it was that cotton firms did not grow to more than middle size between 1800 and 1850.[64]

There have been some broader shifts in emphasis, too. Instead of stressing how *much* had happened by 1851 (whatever the qualifications), it is now commonplace to note how *little* had actually altered (whatever the qualifications). Some studies, explicitly indebted to Wrigley,[k] have stressed how limited and localized were the changes resulting by mid-century.[65] Others have argued that the atypical experience of industrial Lancashire has too frequently been the basis of national generalizations, whereas in fact it was the mercantile and consumer-dominated Home Counties[l] which provided the main stimulus to economic growth.[66] One recent quantitative study has suggested that British economic growth between

1770 and 1815 was about a third slower than was previously supposed; another has reinterpreted the period of 'take-off' as one of stagflation; while a more impressionistic account has questioned the whole notion of a mid-Victorian 'boom'.[67] The view that Britain was the first industrial nation, whose achievements all others consciously emulated, has also been severely undermined, especially in the case of France where, it is now argued, industrialization was taking place in a different way and where, in any case, for much of the eighteenth century, its productivity was higher than Britain's.[68]

This change in emphasis – from what had been accomplished by 1851 to what had not, from 'the take-off into sustained growth' to the 'limits to growth', from national aggregates and sectoral analysis to regional variations and uneven development, from the few large and successful businessmen to the many small and inept entrepreneurs – has now become an orthodoxy so widespread that (like the previous prevailing interpretations) it transcends any claim to be the exclusive preserve of any particular methodology or ideological approach. For example, those of Mathias's collected essays written in the 1970s show a decided shift in emphasis from the argument made in *The First Industrial Nation*. There, the starting-point was development and growth, with the qualifications gradually and carefully made; here, it is the other way round. British growth, he notes, was first, and therefore unlike 'all subsequent case histories'. 'In the 1970's', he continues, we can say 'with some historical assurance' that Britain 'has always been a slow growing economy'. And, elsewhere, there is greater scepticism than before of the work of development economists in so far as they relate to the diffusion of skills, the accumulation and application of capital, diagnoses of poverty and programmes of foreign aid. Ashton's 'influential paragraph' is much less in evidence here than it was a decade earlier.[69]

More generally, A. E. Musson's recent survey explicitly sets out to debunk what he regards as 'the general interpretation presented in most textbooks', namely that 'the industrial revolution had taken place by 1850, that the factory system had triumphed'. This 'older view', that 'it was a sudden, cataclysmic transformation starting around 1760' is, he argues, 'clearly no longer tenable'. Accordingly, he stresses the extent to which consumer goods industries remained handicraft industries, located in small workshops; the degree to which, as shown in the 1851 census, patterns of employment and occupational structure remained dominated by traditional craftsmen, labourers and domestic servants; and the very slow rate at which factories spread and steam power was diffused. 'If', he notes, 'the Industrial Revolution is located in the period 1760–1830, as it frequently is, then there are good grounds for regarding it as the Age of Water Power.' 'British economic historians', he concludes, 'have generally tended to place too much emphasis on the Industrial Revolution of 1750 to 1850. . . . Much of England of 1850 was not very strikingly different from that of 1750.'[70]

V

This is a necessarily compressed account of a long span of history writing, and thus an unavoidably selective summary of a large amount of economic history. The *general* conclusion seems to be that, in accordance with Croce's dictum,[m] economic history *is*, in his sense, contemporary history. Whether they intend to or not, whether they know it or not and whether they like it or not, economic historians write tracts *of* their times and often *for* their times. Rightly or wrongly, contemporaries discerned four readily identifiable phases in the evolution of the British (and, latterly, world) economy since the 1880s; and, during the same hundred years, the four generations of economic history writing on the Industrial Revolution have each evolved a dominant interpretation sufficiently akin to these contemporary perceptions of the economy for it to be more than mere coincidence. The fit is close enough to be remarkable.

This examination of the economic history written yesterday may have some useful implications for the economic history written today and tomorrow. In the first place, it suggests that the dominant interpretation which prevails (albeit not completely) in any given generation is never more than a partial view of that very complex process we inadequately refer to as the Industrial Revolution. In that it draws attention to some important aspect of the subject, it is never going to be wholly 'wrong'; but in that it gives disproportionate emphasis to a

19

limited number of considerations, it is not likely to be wholly 'right', either. So, as today's new generation of economic historians zealously overturns the views of their immediate predecessors, they might ponder whether the old arguments which they assail were ever as all-pervasive or as crude as they are sometimes now made out to have been, and also whether their new formulations are really likely to be any more absolutely 'true' than those which went before. As Ferguson put it in his study of the Renaissance, in words equally applicable to the study of the Industrial Revolution: 'if the historian is to interpret the past at all, he must have a point of view, but he may come closer to objectivity if the point of view is consciously recognized, and not regarded as absolute'.[71] Or, as Supple once put it more briefly: 'It would be a great pity if economic history . . . were to take itself too seriously.'[72]

EDITOR'S NOTES

a Alfred Marshall (1842–1924).
b Between the British and the Afrikaners, 1899–1902.
c Charles Booth published *Life and Labour of the People in London* in 17 volumes between 1891 and 1903. Seebohm Rowntree produced *Poverty: A Study of Town Life* in 1902. Both showed unexpectedly high levels of poverty.
d David Lloyd George (1863–1945) campaigned for land taxes to finance a general welfare programme.
e Reigned between 1820 and 1830.
f A monetary system that allowed for free conversion of currency into gold coin. It tied the money supply closely to the gold supply. Many Britons connected the Gold Standard to English economic supremacy.
g John Maynard Keynes (1883–1946) was one of the great economic thinkers of the twentieth century. He argued for the role of fiscal policies in creating full employment.
h National Economic Development Council.
i The project, directed by the American Secretary of State George Marshall, to provide a massive infusion of capital for European recovery after the Second World War.
j The economist Joseph Schumpeter (1883–1950) studied the role of entrepreneurship in growth.
k E. A. Wrigley, a distinguished economic and demographic historian at Cambridge University.
l The counties around London.
m Benedette Croce, an Italian philosopher of history, coined the phrase, 'All history is contemporary history.'

NOTES

1 A. Toynbee, *Lectures on the Industrial Revolution in England* (London, 1884).
2 D. Fraser, *The Evolution of the British Welfare State* (London, 1973): 124.
3 D. Winch, *Economics and Policy: A Historical Study* (London, 1972): 33–4.
4 B. B. Gilbert, *The Evolution of National Insurance in Great Britain: The Origins of the Welfare State* (London, 1966): 83.
5 Winch, *Economics and Policy*: 34; G. Stedman Jones, *Outcast London: A Study in the Relations between Classes in Victorian Society* (Harmondsworth, 1976): esp. chs 11, 16, 17. But cf. E. P. Hennock, 'Poverty and social theory in England: the experience of the eighteen-eighties', *Social History*, i (1976).
6 S. Hynes, *The Edwardian Turn of Mind* (Princeton, NJ, 1968): 54–69; H. J. Dyos, 'The slums of Victorian London', in his *Exploring the Urban Past: Essays in Urban History* (eds D. Cannadine and D. Reeder) (Cambridge, 1982): 133–9.
7 H. George, *Poverty and Progress* (London, 1883): 6–7.
8 Gilbert, *Evolution of National Insurance*: 77 and ch. 1 *passim*.
9 G. N. Clark, *The Idea of the Industrial Revolution* (Glasgow, 1953): 27.
10 Toynbee, *Lectures on the Industrial Revolution*: 31–2.
11 Lord Milner, 'Reminiscence', in ibid. (1908 edn): xi, xxi.
12 B. Webb, *My Apprenticeship* (London, 1926): 182–3.
13 P. F. Clarke, *Liberals and Social Democrats* (Cambridge, 1978): 154–63, 187–91, 243–52.
14 B. Webb, *My Apprenticeship*: 343–4.
15 ibid.: 348.
16 B. Webb, *Our Partnership* (London, 1948): 147–52. See also V. L. Allen, 'A methodological critique of the Webbs as trade union historians', *Bulletin of the Society for the Study of Labour History*, iv (1962): 4–5.
17 Toynbee, *Lectures on the Industrial Revolution*: 31–2.
18 S. and B. Webb, *The History of Trade Unionism* (London, 1911 edn): 34–5.
19 J. L. and B. Hammond, *The Town Labourer, 1760–1832: The New Civilization* (London, 1917): 3, 98; J. L. and B. Hammond, *The Rise of Modern Industry* (London, 1925): 240.
20 B. Webb, *My Apprenticeship*: 178, 207.
21 Toynbee, *Lectures on the Industrial Revolution*: 83–7.
22 Hammond, *Town Labourer*, chs 10–11, esp. p. 217.
23 S. and B. Webb, *The History of Trade Unionism*: 49–50, 91–2.

24 J. H. Clapham, *An Economic History of Modern Britain*, 3 vols (Cambridge, 1926–38), i, *The Early Railway Age, 1820–1950*: viii, 41, 66, 142, 155.
25 ibid.: vii, 561.
26 ibid.: pp. 315–16.
27 S. and B. Webb, *Decay of Capitalist Civilisation* (London, 1923): 4.
28 M. M. Postan, 'Recent trends in the accumulation of capital', *Economic History Review*, 1st ser., vi (1935): 1.
29 T. E. Gregory, *An Introduction to Tooke and Newmarch's 'A History of Prices and of the State of the Circulation from 1792 to 1856'* (London, 1928): 8.
30 M. M. Postan, *An Economic History of Western Europe, 1945–1964* (London, 1967): 11.
31 D. Landes, *The Unbound Prometheus* (Cambridge, 1969): 498.
32 R. A. Gordon, 'The stability of the US economy', and R. C. O. Matthews, 'Post-war business cycles in the UK', both in M. Bronfenbrenner (ed.), *Is the Business Cycle Obsolete?* (New York, 1969): 4–5, 28, 99, 131–2; F. W. Paish, 'Business Cycles in Britain', *Lloyds Bank Review*, xcviii (1970): 1.
33 M. Gilbert, 'The post-war business cycle in western Europe', *American Economic Review. Papers and Proceedings*, lii (1962): 100–1.
34 Postan, *Economic History of Western Europe*: 18–19.
35 A. Schonfield, *Modern Capitalism* (London, 1965): 62.
36 Gordon, 'Stability of the US economy': 26.
37 Bogdanor and Skidelsky (eds), *Age of Affluence*: introduction, 10–11.
38 Postan, *Economic History of Western Europe*: 25.
39 *The National Plan*, Parliamentary Papers, 1964–5 [Cmd. 2764], xxx: 1; Hutchinson, *Economics and Economic Policy*: 125–30, 207–11; Sir R. Harrod, *Towards a New Economic Policy* (London, 1967): 70.
40 For the background to this, see A. O. Hirschman, 'The rise and fall of development economics', in his *Essays in Trespassing: Economics to Politics and Beyond* (Cambridge, 1981): 7–13. For the early classics of development economics, see N. S. Buchanan and H. S. Ellis, *Approaches to Economic Development* (New York, 1955); H. Leibenstein, *Economic Backwardness and Economic Growth* (New York, 1957); G. M. Meier and R. E. Baldwin, *Economic Development: Prospects, Principles and Policies* (London, 1959); S. Kuznets, *Economic Growth and Structure* (London, 1965).
41 R. E. Cameron, 'Some lessons of history for developing nations', *American Economic Review. Papers and Proceedings*, lviii (1967): 313. Of course, there was, within this shared set of assumptions, a major debate about whether growth should be 'balanced' or 'uneven'. For the two views, see respectively, R. Nurkse, *Problems of Capital Formation in Underdeveloped Countries* (Oxford, 1953); A. O. Hirschman, *The Strategy of Economic Development* (New Haven, Conn., 1958).
42 W. W. Rostow, *The Process of Economic Growth* (Oxford, 1953): 227.
43 W. W. Rostow, *The Process of Economic Growth*, 2nd edn (Oxford, 1960): v–vi, 335. For Rostow's other 'programmatic' books, see W.

W. Rostow, *An American Policy in Asia* (London, 1955): viii, 12–15, ch. 7; W. W. Rostow, *The United States in the World Arena: An Essay in Recent History* (New York, 1960): 432, 444–6, 464; W. W. Rostow, *View from the Seventh Floor* (London, 1964): 1–2, 14, 26, 29.

44 Rostow, *Process of Economic Growth* (2nd edn): 343.

45 W. W. Rostow, *The Stages of Economic Growth: A Non-Communist Manifesto* (Cambridge, 1960): 137. Between 1960 and 1972, *Stages* sold 260,000 copies in the original English version alone. See J. D. Heyl, 'Kuhn, Rostow and Palmer: the problem of purposeful change in the 'sixties', *Historian*, liv (1982): 300 n. 4.

46 Rostow, *Stages of Economic Growth*: 166, 139.

47 R. M. Hartwell, *Industrial Revolution and Economic Growth* (London, 1971): 103–4.

48 W. A. Lewis, *The Theory of Economic Growth* (London, 1955): 265; A. K. Cairncross, *Factors in Economic Development* (London, 1962): 31.

49 C. H. Wilson, 'The entrepreneur in the Industrial Revolution in Britain', *Explorations in Entrepreneurial History*, vii (1955): 132, 134, 138; N. McKendrick, 'Josiah Wedgwood and factory discipline', *Historical Journal*, iv (1961): 51: 'To achieve these ends he demanded complete obedience and complete submission. . . . Of his own energy and devotion there is ample evidence. His energy was remarkable and little daunted him.'

50 R. E. Cameron, *Banking in the Early Stages of Industrialization: A Study in Comparative Economic History* (New York, 1967): ix, 3.

51 P. Deane and H. J. Habakkuk, 'The take-off in Britain', in W. W. Rostow (ed.), *The Economics of Take-Off into Sustained Growth* (London, 1963): esp. 80–2. These findings were incorporated in all the 1960s textbooks. See Landes, *Unbound Prometheus*: 77–9; E. J. Hobsbawm, *Industry and Empire* (Harmondsworth, 1969): 75; Hartwell, *Industrial Revolution and Economic Growth*: 28; P. Deane, *The First Industrial Revolution* (Cambridge, 1965): 107–8, 153–4; P. Mathias, *The First Industrial Nation: An Economic History of Britain 1700–1914* (London, 1969): 3, 13.

52 Deane, *First Industrial Revolution*: 7, 15, 17. See also Landes, *Unbound Prometheus*: 13; Hartwell, *Industrial Revolution and Economic Growth*: 179; Mathias, *First Industrial Nation*: 27, 30, 145.

53 Landes, *Unbound Prometheus*: 105, 118, 120–2; Deane, *First Industrial Revolution*: 150, 255, 263, 270–4; Mathias, *First Industrial Nation*: ch. 9, esp. 259, 263, 271–2.

54 Hartwell, *Industrial Revolution and Economic Growth*: 8, 11, 20. cf. G. R. Elton, *The Practice of History* (London, 1967): 48: 'When some writers can treat pre-industrial England, the economically most advanced society in the Europe of its day, as though it were like tribal Africa or nineteenth-century India, understanding is destroyed, not assisted.'

55 E. E. Schumacher, *Small is Beautiful: A Study of Economics as if People Mattered* (London, 1974): 10–11, 46–7. Since publication, the

book has been through seventeen reprints and sold 750,000 copies in English alone.
56 D. H. Meadows *et al.*, *The Limits to Growth* (New York, 1972): 191. For similar anti-growth views, see D. Bell, *The Cultural Contradictions of Capitalism* (New York, 1976): 237; R. Theobald and S. Mills (eds), *The Failure of Success: Ecological Values vs Economic Myths* (Indianapolis, Indiana, 1973): xii. For a (much less fashionable) restatement of the growth case, see W. Beckerman, *In Defence of Economic Growth* (London, 1974): esp. chs 1, 9.
57 W. W. Rostow, *Getting from Here to There* (New York, 1978): 1–2.
58 W. W. Rostow, *The World Economy: History and Prospect* (Austin, Texas, 1978): 247, 294.
59 Rostow, *Getting from Here to There*: 1, 19, 20.
60 cf. J. K. Galbraith, *Age of Uncertainty* (Boston, Mass., 1977): 280.
61 Rostow, *World Economy*: 383.
62 J. E. Alt, *The Politics of Economic Decline: Economic Management and Political Behaviour in Britain since 1964* (Cambridge, 1979): ch. 2, esp. 33.
63 P. L. Payne, *British Entrepreneurship in the Nineteenth Century* (London, 1974): 24–5, 30–4; S. Marriner, 'English bankruptcy records and statistics before 1850', *Economic History Review*, 2nd ser., xxxiii (1980): 351, 366.
64 V. A. C. Gatrell, 'Labour, power and the size of firms in Lancashire cotton in the second quarter of the nineteenth century', *Economic History Review*, 2nd ser., xxx (1977): 107; S. D. Chapman, 'Financial restraints on the growth of firms in the cotton industry, 1790–1850', *Economic History Review*, 2nd ser., xxxii (1979): 65.
65 W. Ashworth, 'Typologies and evidence: has nineteenth-century Europe a guide to economic growth?', *Economic History Review*, 2nd ser., xxx (1977): 152–4; S. Pollard, *Peaceful Conquest: The Industrialization of Europe, 1760–1970* (Oxford, 1981): vii, 3, 24, 32, 39.
66 C. H. Lee, 'Regional growth and structural change in Victorian Britain', *Economic History Review*, 2nd ser., xxxiv (1981): esp. 450–1; M. Fores, 'The myth of a British Industrial Revolution', *History*, lxvi (1981): 183.
67 C. K. Harley, 'British industrialization before 1841: evidence of slower growth during the Industrial Revolution', *Journal of Economic History*, xlii (1982); J. Mokyr and N. E. Savin, 'Stagflation in historical perspective: the Napoleonic Wars revisited', *Research in Economic History*, i (1976): esp. 199–200: 'the events of the Napoleonic period in England can be usefully compared to our own time'; R. Church, *The Great Victorian Boom, 1850–1873* (London, 1975): 76–8.
68 N. F. R. Crafts, 'Industrial Revolution in England and France: some thoughts on the question "Why Was England First?" ', *Economic History Review*, 2nd ser., xxx (1977): 440; P. K. O'Brien and G. Keyder, *Economic Growth in Britain and France, 1780–1914* (London, 1978): 21, 90, 146–50, 194.

69 P. Mathias, *The Transformation of England* (London, 1979): 10–14, 36, 43, 89–90, 140–2, 146. The essays referred to were first published in 1972, 1973, 1975 and 1976. The point can be made even more forcibly in the light of the recent second edition of the author's textbook: P. Mathias, *First Industrial Nation*, 2nd edn (London, 1983). Many of the earlier references to Third World countries, to development economics and to the value of the British case to those interested in contemporary problems of development have been deleted. cf. pp. 5, 27 and 187 in the first edition with pp. 4, 27 and 167 in the second.
70 A. E. Musson, *The Growth of British Industry* (London, 1978): 8, 62–5, 107–14, 139–42, 149.
71 W. K. Ferguson, *The Renaissance in Historical Thought* (Boston, Mass., 1948): 388.
72 B. Supple, 'Economic history and economic growth', *Journal of Economic History*, xx (1960): 566.

2

MECHANIZATION AND HAND LABOUR IN INDUSTRIALIZING BRITAIN

Raphael Samuel

The distinguished economic historian, David Landes, provided a working definition of the Industrial Revolution which enjoyed universal acceptance. He identifies three areas of fundamental change: '(1) there was a substitution of mechanical devices for human skills; (2) inanimate power – particularly, steam – took the place of human and animal strength; (3) there was a marked improvement in the getting and working of raw materials'.[1] Such is the Industrial Revolution which all textbooks have made familiar.

How relevant was this definition to the lives of millions of nineteenth-century wage-earners? Raphael Samuel questions whether substituting machines for human labour was truly the central feature of nineteenth-century economic development. Demonstrating an impressive grasp of production methods in dozens of trades, the author describes change that was still centred on hand labour and small-scale production. He also explains why progress in mechanization was so uneven. Samuel's case is especially thought-provoking because he examines mid-nineteenth-century Britain, presumably the most successful case of industrial revolution, as Landes defined it.

Readers should ponder the sort of socio-economic transformation Samuel emphasizes. Subsequent essays will follow up on his argument.

Note

1 David Landes, *The Unbound Prometheus* (Cambridge, 1969): 1.

* * *

Whatever their disagreements about the origins of the Industrial Revolution, economic historians are in little doubt about its effects. Steam-power and machinery transformed the labour process, and acted on society as an independent or quasi-independent force, demonic or beneficient according to the point of view, but in any event inescapable. Commodities were cheapened and new markets opened up for them; labour was made enormously more productive at the same time as the physical burden of toil was eased; mechanical ingenuity took the place of handicraft skill. David Landes's summary in *The Unbound Prometheus* is both influential and representative:[1]

> In the eighteenth century, a series of inventions transformed the manufacture of cotton in England and gave rise to a new mode of production – the factory system. During these years, other branches of industry effected comparable advances, and all these together, mutually reinforcing one another, made possible further gains on an ever-widening front. The abundance and variety of these innovations almost defy compilation, but they may be subsumed under three principles: the substitution of machines – rapid, regular, precise, tireless – for human skill and effort; the substitution of inanimate sources of power . . . thereby opening to man a new and almost unlimited supply of energy; the use of new and far more abundant raw materials, in particular, the substitution of mineral for vegetable or animal substances.

This account has the merit of symmetry, but the notion of substitution is problematic, since in many cases there are no real equivalents to compare. The fireman raising steam in an engine cab, or the boiler-maker flanging plates in a furnace, were engaged in wholly new occupations which had no real analogy in previous times. So too, if one thinks of the operations they were called upon to perform, rather than the nature of the finished product, were the mill-hands of Lancashire and the West Riding.[a] And if one looks at technology from the point of view of labour rather than that of capital, it is a cruel caricature to represent machinery as dispensing with toil. High-pressure engines had their counterpart in high-pressure work, endless chain mechanisms in non-stop jobs. And quite apart from the demands which machinery itself imposed there was a huge army of labour engaged in supplying it with raw materials, from the slave labourers on the cotton plantations of the United States to the tinners and copper-miners of Cornwall. The Industrial Revolution, so far from abridging human labour, created a whole new world of labour-intensive jobs: railway navvying is a prime example, but one could consider too the puddlers and shinglers in the rolling mills, turning pig-iron into bars, the alkali workers stirring vats of caustic soda and a whole spectrum of occupations in what the factory legislation of the 1890s was belatedly to recognize as 'dangerous' trades. Working pace was transformed in old industries as well as new, with slow and cumbersome methods of production giving way, under the pressure of competition, to overwork and sweating.[b]

Nor is it possible to equate the new mode of production with the factory system. Capitalist enterprise took quite different forms in, for instance, cabinet-making and the clothing trades, where rising demand was met by a proliferation of small producers. In agriculture and the fisheries it depended upon an increase in numbers rather than the concentration of production under one roof. In metalwork and engineering[c] – at least until the 1880s – it was the workshop rather than the factory which prevailed, in boot and shoemaking, cottage industry. The distributive trades rested on the broad shoulders of carmen and dockers, the electric telegraph on the juvenile runner's nimble feet. Capitalist growth was rooted in a subsoil of small-scale enterprise. It depended not on one technology but on many, and made use, too, of a promiscuous variety of profit-making devices, from the adulteration of soot[2] (in which there was an international trade with the West Indies, as well as a local one with farmers for manure)[3] to the artificial colouring of smoked haddocks.[4]

LABOUR POWER

Capitalism in the nineteenth century grew in various ways. Mechanization in one department of production was often complemented by an increase of sweating in others; the growth of large firms by a proliferation of small producing units; the concentration of production in factories by the spread of outwork in the home. Sugar was refined in factories, like Messrs

Tate and Lyle's at Silvertown;[5] but sweets were manufactured for the million in back-street kitchens and courts, as also were such popular children's purchases as ginger beer, sarsaparilla and ice-cream (among the manufacturers, in 1890s East London, were out-of-work dockers, victimized by the employers as a result of their activities in the dock strike).[6] Timber was sawn at the saw mills, where steam-driven machinery was, by the 1850s, very general; but it was shaped at the carpenter's bench, on the cabinet-maker's tressles and at the cooper's coke-fired cresset. In ironmaking, the giant furnaces of the Black Country existed cheek-by-jowl with thousands of backyard smithies, complementary in their action, yet radically distinct. The same was true of steelmaking and the cutlery trades in Sheffield, where thirty or forty rolling mills supplied the working material of some sixty handicraft trades in which production was organized by outworking journeymen-masters.[7] Textiles were mechanized and accounted for far more steam-power than any other trade, but the clothing trades, which increased by leaps and bounds in the 1840s and 1850s, depended on the poor needlewoman's fingers.

The most complete triumph of the machine was in the cotton trade of industrial Lancashire. Elsewhere its progress was more halting, and there were major sectors of the economy where down to the 1870s steam-power had made very little impression at all. Often its effects were secondary, applying only to the preparatory process of manufacture – or to the finishing – while leaving the main body of the work untouched: the case, for example, with firebricks.[8] In other instances it served to make handicraft labour more productive without impairing its skill – as in the example of glass-cutting, where steam-power turned the grinding wheels, previously worked by a man or boy assistant, but the delicate work of grinding, smoothing and polishing remained in the hands of the craftsman who had traditionally performed it.[9] In yet other instances steam-power and machinery were chemical rather than mechanical in their action, and fuel-saving rather than labour-saving in effect. This was the case, in ironmaking, with Neilson's Hot Blast, which cut down coal consumption by about a half,[10] and in glassmaking Siemens's tank furnace. Even when machinery was extensively applied it by no means necessarily reduced workers to the status of mere hands; often its role was ancillary rather than commanding, and it may be useful to suggest a broad line of distinction between the textile industries on the one hand where, by mid-Victorian times, repetition work largely prevailed, and metalwork and engineering on the other, where the production process was discontinuous, and depended on craftsmanly skill. Mechanization and steam-power, in short, were by no means inseparably linked, and a vast amount of nineteenth-century work was affected by them only at second or third remove.

In coal-mining, steam-power transformed the scale of operations, while leaving the technology of hewing unchanged. Steam-driven fans were applied to ventilation, and allowed working places to proliferate, instead of being tied to the foot of the shaft. Steam-driven pumps were applied to underground drainage, and allowed the mining engineers to explore new and deeper levels, more especially in the second half of the century, as the shallower seams showed signs of exhaustion. But there was a total absence of mechanization at the point of production, where the coal was still excavated by shovel and pick – 'tools of the most primitive description, requiring the utmost amount of bodily exertion to render effective'.[11] Mechanical coal-cutters were frequently patented and in times of strike high hopes were entertained by employers of the 'revolution' they might affect,[12] but in 1901, forty years after the first wave of patents, only 1½ per cent of total output could be attributed to them[13] – a percentage which had still only risen to 8½ in 1913.[14] Output was increased not by mechanization but by recruiting extra men. More and more hewers were needed as workings were extended both laterally and in depth. The numbers of hauliers (mainly boys) also increased: there was more coal for them to handle, and longer galleries to travel. Longer galleries also meant more roofs to prop, more roads to keep up, more rails to be laid down, while the increased use of blasting meant more hand-bored holes. The nineteenth century saw the creation of whole new classes of underground worker – 'stonemen' or rippers who had the job of extending the levels, timbermen to do the propping,[15] shotfirers to bore the holes. The mining labour force, which had stood at little over 200,000 in 1841 rose to 1,202,000 by 1911.[16] Animal power, too, was brought to production's aid, with the introduction of pit ponies for underground haulage: there were an estimated 11,000 of them in 1851, 25,000 in 1881, 70,000 by 1911.[17]

Food processing in mid-Victorian England was perhaps less subject to technological improvement than any other branch of production. Vegetables were dressed for the market by hand. Earth-stained crops, such as celery and radishes, were washed and bunched by women and children, working for market gardeners in their sheds.[18] At Covent Garden, peas were podded in the market itself and sold 'ready for the saucepan' according to their respective size (the work was chiefly in the hands of old women, working at the rate of 1s. or 18d a day and recruited by salesmen from the local workhouse).[19] Pickling, too, though increasingly a factory trade, was mostly done by hand. The vegetables had to be soaked in brine, diced or sliced to size, liberally sprinkled with vinegar and then 'artistically arranged' in jars.[20] It was cold winter work (the vegetables had to be kept in the cold for fear that they would rot) and chapped hands and cuts are remembered occupational hazards.[21] Onions were particularly labour-intensive as they had to be individually peeled. 'Consequently in a bottle of pickles every onion is always visible from the outside though perhaps a cabbage may fill up the middle – an onion is never allowed to enjoy oblivion.' There was more machinery in jam-making, where by the 1880s steam-jacketed boilers reduced the fruit to pulp, but the preparatory stages were performed by hand. The fruits were sorted out into their respective qualities and the damaged parts cut away, oranges peeled, lemons squeezed, soft fruit separated from brambles. Extra labour was taken on at the jam factories during the height of the fruit-picking season, and sacked when it was over.[22]

The building industry, like mining and agriculture, was labour-intensive and increased output was achieved by putting on extra men: the workforce recorded in the census was 376,000 in 1841, by 1901 it had risen to 1,216,000. Building and construction was one of the fastest-growing sectors of the economy in mid-Victorian times, and accounted for between 20 and 30 per cent of gross domestic fixed capital formation, rather more than twice the amount attributed to cotton.[23] But the scale of enterprise was characteristically small, and investment, whether by master-builders or subcontractors, went on labour and materials, not on plant. The main thrust of technical

31

innovation, such as it was, came in the direction of labour-saving materials rather than of mechanical devices. In the 1850s and 1860s their influence was comparatively slight. The painter still mixed his own colours; bricklayers still cut and shaped their own bricks (so late as 1874 it was considered a more important part of their work than setting); carpenters and joiners worked, very often, to their own designs.[24]

In the leather trades, every process of production, from the preparatory work to the finishing, depended on manual dexterity and strength. The industry employed some quarter of a million people in the 1830s and McCulloch, in his *Statistical Account* of 1837, estimated it as third or fourth in the kingdom, 'inferior only . . . to . . . cotton, wool, and iron'. But then and down to a much later date the peculiar nature of its raw material seemed to make it impervious to the machine. 'I do not think you will ever get machinery into our trade', a clicker told the Royal Commission on Labour in 1892, 'until you can grow all the animals of one size with just the same blemishes'. Tanning (the preparation of leather from raw hides) was a dirty business, and for the yardsmen who had the job of lugging heavy animal carcasses in and out of pits, it was also a wet one, which needed a strong constitution (in Bermondsey, Mayhew tells us, the majority were Irish). The hide took a tremendous beating when it was not soaking in the pits. The flesher and the unhairer slashed away at it with their pokes and knives, the shedman pummelled it with a double-headed stave, while at the end of the process the creases were taken out of the leather by a triangular steel pin, with a labourer's weight behind it. Tanning was a protracted process, though the period varied according to the stoutness of the hide, and the manufacture for which it was destined: in the case of sole leather it could take a year or more to complete. Patent improvements abridged the period of the work ('almost every tanner has some process peculiar to his establishment') but they did not alter its essential character. Even in such a large tannery as the Avonside works of Messrs Evans, 'the most modern and complete' in the Bristol region, according to the *Boot and Shoe Trade Journal* in 1887, it took more than twelve months for a hide to progress through the successive stages of its treatment. The firm used a Tangye pump for pumping water; there was a machine for grinding bark; and there were three boilers, though more than one was rarely used at a time. But beyond these the sound of machinery was 'scarcely heard'.

In wood, as in leather, the variability of the raw material, and the delicacy, in many cases, of the finished product, made mechanization problematical, and, as in the case of shoemaking, there was a superabundance of labour ready to take up new openings on the basis of handicraft skill. Economic growth took place almost independently of the machine. Steam-power was applied at the saw mills, turning timber into deals, or slicing them up thinly as veneers. And in the 1860s and 1870s steam joineries began to appear, supplying ready-made mouldings and parts. But woodworkers themselves, with the exception of the sawyers, were only indirectly affected by these changes.

In metallurgy steam-power was massively harnessed to the primary processes of production, notably in puddling and rolling; but at the same time new fields were opened up for handicraft skills. In foundry work machine moulding[d] was introduced in the 1850s (during the lock-out of 1852 some engineering employers fondly believed that it would deliver them from their men),[25] but it remained confined to the most inferior branches of the trade, such as the making of cast-iron drain-pipes.[26] Moulders – 'the wildest, the most grimy, the most independent, and, unfortunately, the most drunken and troublesome of any English workmen who have any claim to the title of "skilled" '[27] were virtually untouched by it and for the most part worked with the very simplest of tools, whilst their brethren, the dressers, smoothed the rough castings with hand-files.[28] The Friendly Society of Iron-moulders was composed uniquely of handicraft workers right down to the 1900s and (as employers complained) maintained a high rate of wages, restrictive shop practices and unsleeping hostility to the machine-based class of worker.[29]

COMBINED AND UNEVEN DEVELOPMENT

The foregoing epitome, though necessarily abbreviated, may be enough to suggest that in speaking of the primacy of labour power one is referring not to single instances, or to curious survivals, but to a dominant pattern of growth. In manufacture, as in agriculture and mineral work, a vast amount of capitalist enterprise was organized on the basis of hand rather than steam-powered technologies. In Marxist terms, the labour process was dependent on the strength, skill, quickness and sureness of touch of the individual worker rather than upon the simultaneous and repetitive operations of the machine. The restraints 'inseparable from human labour power'[30] has not yet been cast aside. On the contrary, a great deal of entre- preneurial ingenuity was employed in turning them to advan- tage. Commercial progress depended quite largely on the physical adaptability of the worker, whether it involved crawl- ing on all fours to gather the woad harvest,[31] climbing up and down perpendicular ladders (in a Cornish tin mine the ascent would take an hour or more each day)[32] or working, like boiler- makers on repair jobs, upside down in tanks.[33] The lungs of the glass-blower, working as bellows, or those of the gas-fitter, soldering pipes, were not the least of the forces of production which nineteenth-century capitalism summoned to its aid, nor were there any more important in the clothing trades than the needlewoman's fingers and thumbs. In the Potteries, dinner plates were shaped by dextrous jerks of the flat-presser's wrists, and surfaces varnished with the dipper's bare arms in a glaze tub (in 1861 Dr Greenhow estimated they were immersed for 8 of a 12-hour-day). Ironmaking depended on violent muscular exertion, and an ability to withstand white heat, engineering on precision of judgement and touch. In the metalworking trades no action was more highly valued than the ability to deliver well-directed blows with the hammer, while those engaged in press-work were in almost perpetual motion with their arms and wrists: 'practiced workers' in the metal button trade were said to make from 14,000 to 20,000 strokes a day, 'the whole strength of a woman' being needed on the heavier class of press.[34]

The slow progress of mechanization in mid-Victorian times had many different causes, but one of them was undoubtedly the relative abundance of labour, both skilled and unskilled. In striking contrast to the earlier years of the Industrial Revo- lution, every branch of employment was over-stocked. In agri- culture there was a huge labour surplus, men, women and children who never had full employment except in the harvest months. Railway building and construction sites depended upon a great army of freelance, tramping navvies, who took up employment only for the duration of a job. The reserve army of labour was no less a feature of the workshop trades. The supply of needlewomen was infinitely elastic – the number recorded in the census tripled between 1841 and 1861 – whilst that of carpentry and joiners, tailors and shoemakers, printers and bookbinders was always far greater than the number of regular berths. 'Tramping artisans'[e] were very much a feature of the labour market in the new industrial crafts, such as boiler-making.[35] In iron shipbuilding, where most employment was on a job-and-finish basis[f] they constituted the bulk of the labour force: Samuel Kydd in 1858 described the Clydeside shipbuilders, restlessly scouring the riverside for work, as being more like 'wandering tinkers' than regular mechanics.[36] The trade union records of the mid-Victorian ironmoulders show that there were seldom less than 5 per cent of members out of work, and often more than 10 per cent.[37]

Another reason for the slow progress of mechanization was the possibility of increasing productivity within a hand technology, either by the introduction of improved tools, or by a more systematic exploitation of labour, or both. Agriculture provides a prime example, with the change from sickle to the scythe, the extension of soil-improving crops and manures and the mid-Victorian improvements in field drainage. Coal-mining, too, advanced on the basis of improved hand technology. Between 1850 and 1880 output in the industry doubled, and this was due not only to the increase in the number of underground workers, but also to improved haulage methods, harder work and improvements in the miner's pick, with the substitution of steel for iron.[38] At the same time better transport, both by sea and land, helped to end local monopolies, and brought down prices to the industrial and domestic consumer. Another striking example, to which Eric Hobsbawm drew attention some years ago, is that of gas-making, an industry which down to almost the end of the century was entirely dependent on the physical strength of the stokers. The amount of coal carbonized in the London gasworks rose by some 75 per cent between 1874 and 1888, while the labour force increased by under a third.

A third alternative to mechanization – and another avenue to more rapid workmanship – was the division of labour and simplification of the individual task. In mid-Victorian times it was just as likely to take place off the master's premises as on them. A prime example is the introduction of 'riveting' in the boot and shoe trade which brought a new and cheaper class of boot on to the market, and revolutionized the wholesale trade. Under the new system of work the soles were nailed to the uppers, instead of being stitched, and the work of 'making', previously performed by one man, was now divided between two – the riveters and the finishers.[39] Riveting was a spectacular commercial success, and Leicester, where the invention was patented in 1861, rapidly established itself as the largest producer of ready-made footwear.[40] Skill was reduced, labour costs fell and there was a sharp increase in productivity. 'The old crafts would make about three boots or two pairs a day . . . the riveter and finisher can produce ten pairs in the same time.'[41] The new labour, however, was unmistakably handicraft in character.

> No machinery was used; the soles and uppers were cut by hand, then the upper was moulded round a last, with the edges pulled inwards. A 'nailer' or 'riveter', as he was variously called, would fill his mouth with 'sprigs', and taking them one by one would hammer on the sole and heel. When this had been done, the edges were trimmed with a sharp knife. Finally, the sole and edges were . . . polished with a hot iron and a heelball.[42]

Another obstacle to mechanization was the gap between expectation and performance. In many cases the machines failed to perform the 'self-acting' miracles promised in the patents, and either needed a great deal of skilled attendance, or failed to execute their appointed tasks. Even if brought 'nearly . . . to perfection'[43] by its inventor, a machine would often prove difficult to operate. Unexpected snags would be encountered, unintended effects would appear and it was possible for patent to follow patent without anything like continuous flow production being achieved. Wright's pin machine of 1824, which, according to its promoters, 'during a single revolution . . . produced a perfect pin',[44] turned out to be so far from perfect that forty years later, despite thousands of pounds spent on costly experiments, the 'nobbing' or heading of the pin had still very often to be done by hand (in Gloucester this was a cottage industry, though the body of the pin was made in factories).[45]

Wall's 1880 machine for manufacturing cheap pottery failed more quickly, though causing a brief sensation among the operatives. 'There was one defect in nearly all the ware independent of the want of polishing; air cracks almost invariably made their appearance in the backs of the ware after firing.'[46] The steam-powered 'Jolly', which had caused such a panic in the Potteries thirty-five years earlier (the Potters' Union set up an Emigration Society, and planted a colony in America, as a way of escaping it)[47] failed 'partly, it is supposed, through the desire of the employers not to come into conflict with the men', but chiefly 'owing to some defects in . . . construction'.[48] (Later it resurfaced, and by the 1890s was in general use.)[49]

Another obstacle to mechanization was the irregular nature of demand, and its often limited character. Steam-power and machinery were only profitable if they were geared to large-scale production. But in the workshop trades short production runs were endemic, and output fluctuated sharply not only with the trade cycle, but also from season to season and in many cases from week to week. 'Little makers' like the Willenhall locksmiths, the Sheffield cutlers or the cabinet-makers of Bethnal Green, could only afford to make up goods in small quantities at a time, because they had to meet wages and costs out of weekly earnings. Warehousemen and buyers-up, for their part, were niggardly in their purchases, and preferred, as a matter of policy, to trade from week to week rather than to run the risk of carrying unsold stock on their hands. Consumer demand also tended to favour limited production runs, alternating between periods of heavy pressure, when there was a helter-skelter rush of work (as in the 'bull' weeks immediately preceding Christmas) and others when trade was dead.[50] In conditions like these it was easier, when faced with a rush of orders, to take on extra hands, or subcontract the work, than to install expensive machinery and plant: less risky in the long run, and in the short run at least a great deal more profitable.

The position was not necessarily different in heavy industry, despite the vast scale of many works. Tin plates – the most recent historian of the south Wales industry tells us – 'were not manufactured ahead of demand but were rolled to order'.[51] According to Menelaus, the manager of the Dowlais Works, this was also very frequently the case in heavy iron. 'When rolled iron is wanted either in large masses, or of difficult sections and . . . lengths', he told the south Wales Institute of Engineers in 1860, 'the quantities generally are so small that even if you have suitable machinery, before you get properly to work . . . the order is finished'.[52] In shipbuilding and engineering, a great deal of work was done to order rather than for stock, while the willingness of British engineering firms to make large numbers of products in small quantities – and to fit them up, if necessary, on site – was the very basis of the worldwide reputation for excellence they enjoyed.[53]

CONCLUSION

Steam-power and hand technology may represent different principles of industrial organization, and to the historian they may well appear as belonging to different epochs, the one innovatory, the other 'traditional' and unchanging in its ways. But from the point of view of nineteenth-century capitalist development they were two sides of the same coin, and it is fitting that the Great Exhibition of 1851 – 'the authentic voice of British capitalism in the hour of its greatest triumph'[54] – should have given symbolic representation to them both. 'Steam power', an admiring commentator noted, 'wholly turned the mahogany which runs round the galleries of the Crystal Palace'.[55] But the 300,000 panes of glass which covered it were blown by hand,[56] and so was the Crystal Fountain which formed the centre-piece of the transept, 'glittering in all the colours of the rainbow'.[57] The promoters were intoxicated with the idea of 'self-acting machinery', and the technological miracles it might perform. But they devoted a great deal of their space to – among other things – needlework; and in demonstrating the competitive capabilities of British industry they were heavily dependent on artisan skills. Most of the manufactures on display were handicraft products, and even in the Machinery Court many of the exhibits were assembled from hand-made components.

The orthodox account of the Industrial Revolution concentrates on the rise of steam-power and machinery, and the spread of the factory system. It has much less to say about alternative forms of capitalist enterprise (such as those to be found in mining and quarrying), about the rise of sweating or the spread of backyard industries and trades. Nor does it tell us much about the repercussions of technology on work. Landes's picture has the compelling power of paradigm, with mechanization on an 'ever-widening front' and steam-power – 'rapid, regular, precise' – effortlessly perfoming labour's tasks. But if one looks at the economy as a whole rather than at its most novel and striking features, a less orderly canvas might be drawn – one bearing more resemblance to a Bruegel or even a Hieronymus Bosch[g] than to the geometrical regularities of a modern abstract. The industrial landscape would be seen to be full of diggings and pits as well as of tall factory chimneys. Smithies would sprout in the shadows of the furnaces, sweatshops in those of the looms. Agricultural labourers might take up the foreground, armed with sickle or scythe, while behind them troops of women and children would be bent double over the ripening crops in the field, pulling charlock, hoeing nettles or cleaning the furrows of stones. In the middle distance there might be navvies digging sewers and paviours laying flags. On the building sites there would be a bustle of man-powered activity, with house-painters on ladders and slaters nailing roofs. Carters would be loading and unloading horses, market women carrying baskets of produce on their heads, dockers balancing weights. The factories would be hot and steamy, with men stripped to the singlet, and juvenile runners in bare feet. At the lead works women would be carrying pots of poisonous metal on their heads, in the bleachers' shed they would be stitching yards of chlorined cloth, at a shoddy mill sorting rags. Instead of calling his picture 'machinery' the artist might prefer to name it 'toil'.

Nineteenth-century capitalism created many more skills than it destroyed, though they were different in kind from those of the all-round craftsmen, and subject to a wholly new level of exploitation. The change from sail to steam in shipping led to the rise of a whole number of new industrial crafts, as well as providing a wider arena for the exercise of old ones. The same may be said of the shift from wood to iron in vehicle building, and of horse to steam in transport. In the woodworking trades a comparatively small amount of machinery supported a vast proliferation of handicraft activities, while in metallurgy the cheapening of manufacturing raw materials led to a multiplication of journeymen-masters. The mid-Victorian engineer[h] was a tool-bearer rather than a machine minder; the boiler-maker was an artisan rather than a factory hand. In coal-mining activity increased by the recruitment of a vast new class of workers who were neither exactly labourers, nor yet artisans, but who very soon laid claim to hereditary craft skills. Much the same was true of workers in the tin-plate mills and ironworks. The number of craftsmen in the building trade increased by leaps and bounds, though the rise of new special-ities led to a narrowing of all-round skills.

In juxtaposing hand and steam-powered technologies one is speaking of a *combined* as well as of an *uneven* development. In mid-Victorian times, as earlier in the nineteenth century, they represented *concurrent* phases of capitalist growth, feeding on one another's achievements, endorsing one another's effects. Both were exposed to the same market forces; both depended for their progress upon the mobilization of wage-labour on a hitherto unprecedented scale; and both were equally subject to the new work discipline, though it affected them in different ways. The Industrial Revolution rested on a broad handicraft basis, which was at once a condition of its development and a restraint on its further growth.

EDITOR'S NOTES

a Areas where early factory development was most pronounced.
b Refers to conditions of work characterized by piece-rates and low-quality production. As rates fall, workers have to labour ever harder to earn the same income.
c Machine-building industry.
d Pouring molten metal into moulds which gave it the desired form.
e Term used to characterize the traditional itinerancy of artisans, who often travelled from job to job.
f Employment which lasted only long enough to complete a particu-lar task.
g Painters of the sixteenth century who are known for canvases that portrayed disorderliness and grotesqueness.
h Mechanic.

NOTES

Reprinted from 'The workshop of the world: steam power and hand technology in mid-Victorian Britain' in *History Workshop*, 3: 6–72 (spring 1977) by permission of Oxford University Press.

MECHANIZATION AND HAND LABOUR

1 David Landes, *The Unbound Prometheus* (Cambridge, 1969): 41.
2 George Elson, *The Last of the Climbing Boys* (London, 1900): 78–81; Charles Booth Manuscripts, the London School of Economics: B 160, fol. 16.
3 *Liverpool Mercury* (10 October 1845): 400.
4 Henry Mayhew, *London Labour and the London Poor* (London, 1861).
5 W. Glenny Crory, *East London Industries* (London, 1876).
6 Charles Booth Manuscripts: A. 24 part A, fols 17–23; B. 10, fol. 125; B. 16, fols 43, 91; B. 44, fols 26, 41; B. 45, fols 60, 147.
7 *Parliamentary Papers* (hereafter *PP*) (1876) (*c.* 1443–1) XXX, Rep . . . Fact. & Workshops Act, QQ 12058–61; Frank Hill, 'Combinations in Sheffield', *Trade Societies and Strikes* (London, 1860): 564–5.
8 *PP* (1876), XXX, Rep . . . Fact. & Workshops Act, QQ 5529, 5644; Webb Collection, the London School of Economics: sect. A, vol. X, fol. 386; A. B. Searle, *Refractory Materials* (London, 1917): 144.
9 *Morning Chronicle* (Birmingham, 23 December 1850).
10 Ellis A. Davidson, *Our Houses* (London, 1869): 96; Prof. Barff, 'Glass and silicates', in George Bevan (ed.), *British Manufacturing Industries*, 14 vols (London, 1876), 7: 76–7.
11 C. W. Waring, 'On the application of machinery to cutting coal', *Transactions of South Wales Institute of Engineers*, III (1862–3): 95.
12 *Manchester Examiner* (26 July 1865): 5, cols 2–3; cf. also *Barnsley Chronicle* (September 1866); *Capital and Labour* (15 April 1874); *Iron and Coal Trades Review* (15 May 1872): 386.
13 J. E. Williams, *The Derbyshire Miners* (London, 1962): 174.
14 H. J. Habakkuk, *American and British Technology in the Nineteenth Century* (Cambridge, 1962): 200.
15 In earlier years the hewers had been expected to do their own propping, but in the second half of the nineteenth century they were vigorously resisting this because it cut down on their piece-rate earnings. *The Times* (5 July 1873): 5; *Iron and Coal Trades Review* (13 March 1872).
16 B. R. Mitchell and Phyllis Deane, *Abstract of British Historical Statistics* (Cambridge, 1971): 60, 119.
17 F. M. L. Thompson, 'Nineteenth-century horse sense', *Economic History Review* 2nd ser., XXIX, I, appendix (1976): 80.
18 Charles Whitehead, 'Report . . . market garden competition', *Journal of the Royal Agricultural Society* (1879): 841, 848; Charles Whitehead, *Market Gardening for Farmers* (London, 1880): 12.
19 Andrew Wynter, *Curiosities of Civilization* (London, 1860): 235; C. W. Shaw, *The London Market Gardens* (London, 1879): 159–60.
20 Oral history: interviews of the writer with Mrs Annie McClough of Liverpool, April 1972.
21 Charles Booth Manuscripts: B. 117, 34.
22 Charles Booth, *London Life and Labour* 1st ser., IV (London, 1904): 288–9.
23 R. A. Church, *The Great Victorian Boom, 1850–1873* (London, 1975): 34.

24 E. Dobson, *Rudiments of the Art of Building* (London, 1849): 25, 42–3, 261.
25 H. J. Fryth and Henry Collins, *The Foundry Workers* (Manchester, 1959): 44.
26 Andrew Ure, *Dictionary of Arts, Manufactures, and Mines*, 3 vols (London, 1860), II: 203.
27 *Recollections of English Engineers* (London, 1868): 218.
28 Ure, *Dictionary*.
29 For the trade union, Fyrth and Collins, *Foundry Workers*; for the restrictive practices, *Capital and Labor* (April 1874); W. G. Riddell, *Adventures of an Obscure Victorian* (London, 1932): 33–6; Charles Booth Manuscripts: B. 89 fol. 55.
30 Karl Marx, *Capital*, 2 vols (London, 1949), 1.
31 Norman T. Willis, *Woad in the Fens* (Lincoln, 1970); J. B. Hurry, *The Woad Plant and its Dye* (Oxford, 1930).
32 *PP* (1861) (161) XVI, 3rd rep. M. O. Privy C.: 130–1; *PP* (1864) (3389) XXIV, Comm. on non-inspected Mines: xiii, xiv–xv.
33 Alfred Williams, *Life in a Railway Factory* (London, 1915): 115.
34 J. S. Wright, 'On the employment of women in factories in Birmingham', *Transactions of the National Association of Social Science* (1857): 539–40.
35 E. J. Hobsbawm, 'The tramping artisan', in his *Labouring Men* (London, 1964) is the fundamental article on this subject.
36 Samuel Kydd, 'The condition of the people', Goldsmith Collection (University of London): fol. 88.
37 Fryth and Collins, *Foundry Workers*: 44 n; Howell Collection, Bishopgate Institute, Friendly Society of Iron Founders, *Annual Report* (1887): 10.
38 Church, *Great Victorian Boom*: 44; A. J. Taylor, 'Labour productivity and technical innovation in the coal industry 1859–1914', *Economic History Review*, 2nd ser., XIV (1961).
39 Alan Fox, *A History of the National Union of Boot and Shoe Trade Operatives* (Oxford, 1958): 14–15.
40 C. P. R. Mountfield, 'The footware industry of the East Midlands', *East Midlands Geographer*, IV, I (1966).
41 *Boot and Shoe Trade Journal*, XXVII (23 April 1892): 535.
42 *Oliver's, 1869–1950* (Leicester, 1950): 8; Northampton Reference Library, *Recollections of William Arnold*: 20–3.
43 *Pottery Gazette*, VI (1 April 1882): 343.
44 Thomas Phipson, 'The pin industry', in Samuel Timmins (ed.), *The Industrial Resources of Birmingham and the Midland Hardware District* (London, 1866): 601; S. R. H. Jones, 'Price associations and competition in the British pin industry', *Economic History Review*, 2nd ser., XXVI, 2 (1973); Ure, *Dictionary*, III: 458–9.
45 C. Violet Butler, 'Pins', in William Page (ed.) *Victoria County History of Gloucestershire* 11 vols (London, 1907), II: 207.
46 *Pottery Gazette*, VI (1 April 1882): 343; Harold Owen, *The Staffordshire Potter* (London, 1901): 311.

47 Owen, *Staffordshire Potter*: 63–71; An Old Potter, *When I Was a Child* (London, 1903): 186–7.
48 S. J. Thomas, 'Pottery', in F. Galton (ed.), *Workers on their Industry* (London, 1895): 191.
49 *Pottery Gazette* (1 November 1879): 428; *Pottery and Glass Trades Gazette*, V (April 1881): 305.
50 Public Record Office, HO 45/9833 /B 9744/2; *Labour News* (28 November 1874, 2 January 1875); *Ironmonger*, II (31 December 1860): 209, V (31 December 1863): 353.
51 W. E. Minchinton, *The British Tinplate Industry, a History* (Oxford, 1957): 40.
52 Menelaus, 'On rolling heavy iron', *Transactions of South Wales Institute of Engineers*, II (1860–1): 78.
53 Roderick Floud, *The British Machine-Tool Industry 1850–1914* (Cambridge, 1976): 51, 55–6, 67.
54 Francis Klingender, *Art and the Industrial Revolution* (London, 1975): 144.
55 George Dodd, *Curiosities of Industry* (London, 1852): 18.
56 G. M. L. Strauss *et al.*, *England's Workshops* (London, 1864): 186.
57 *Illustrated Exhibitor* (7 June 1851).

3

SOCIAL CHANGE IN MODERN EUROPE: THE BIG PICTURE

Charles Tilly

By the end of the 1960s, the economic historians whom Cannadine analysed ceased being the principal interpreters of industrial Europe. The strongest intellectual currents of the day called for history 'from below' – that is, with the perspective of ordinary people in mind. The populist thrust gave considerable momentum to the 'new labour history', which took as its agenda investigating the thoughts, experiences and collective action of working people.[1] Charles Tilly emerged as one of the most prolific and influential voices for this sort of social history. It is not surprising that Tilly has made one of the most ambitious attempts to replace the Industrial Revolution paradigm with other ways of thinking about large-scale socio-economic change.

Readers must come to this essay with a grasp of Tilly's basic concepts. He believes that two forces have had the greatest impact on the lives of ordinary people, the growth of capitalism and the extension of state power.[2] By capitalism Tilly does not merely mean industrial development. Capitalism is an economic system based on non-coercive wage-labour. He would insist that merchants practised capitalism every bit as much as factory owners did, and much earlier. Indeed, Tilly stresses the transforming capacity of commercial capitalism. By 'state', Tilly means the central political unit. Tilly is particularly interested in its expanding capacity to tax, draft, sequester and otherwise compel obedience.

Also central to Tilly's overview is the concept of proletarianization. Tilly defines it as 'a set of processes that increase the number of people who lack control over the mean of production and who survive by selling labor power'.[3] Tilly hypothesizes that the growth of capitalism and of the state increased the portion of the population which had lost control over the means of production (their own land, looms, tools, etc.) and which had to work for wages. In Tilly's view, prolet-

arianization brought dire consequences for the millions who experienced it. The demotion to wage-labourers reduced the likelihood that children would have an economic enterprise to take over from the parents, swelled the number of those who had to purchase life's necessities and made millions ever more vulnerable to marked price swings. Finally, it turned self-employed people into proletarians – but not necessarily in factories.

This wide-ranging essay makes an excellent case for a new description of socio-economic changes. The new description does not feature the Industrial Revolution. Students should note the chronology Tilly proposes – the conventional dates of the Industrial Revolution, 1760–1840, mean little to him. They should also consider the faults of an analysis which takes the form 'before/after the Industrial Revolution'. Most important, readers should ponder how Tilly squares a recognition of substantial economic change in the nineteenth century with the claim that the Industrial Revolution was an 'illusion'.

Notes

1 The 'old' labour history concentrated on political parties, ideologies and trade unions, mainly from the leaders' point of view.
2 Tilly explains this position clearly in *The Contentious French* (Cambridge, Mass., 1986).
3 *As Sociology Meets History* (New York, 1981): 179.

* * *

As a result of recent decades' work in social history, our picture of general changes in European life over the last few centuries has altered greatly. Not long ago, historians thought, and taught, a Europe peopled mainly by an immobile, traditional peasant mass, dominated by church and state, which broke apart after 1750 with an industrial revolution followed by a series of democratic revolutions.

Witness the 1950 edition of Robert R. Palmer's first-rate survey, *A History of the Modern World*.[1] Palmer's presentation of modern Europe outside of Italy begins with the fifteenth-century New Monarchs (Henry VII, Louis XI and others) who established royal power and stable government, and thus laid a political foundation for a commercial revolution. The commercial revolution includes an expansion of cottage industry, in which rural people produced at home on orders from local merchants. As a result of rising prices, peasants prospered and landlords faltered in western Europe; in eastern Europe, however, landlords themselves retained control of production, thereby taking advantage of price rises while subordinating manorial workers to their personal control.

Palmer's reconstruction continues: as monarchs fortified their states for war, conquest and internal control, worldwide exploration and the growth of scientific thinking combined to generate prosperity and modern ways:

> the greatest social development of the eighteenth century, with the possible exception of the progress of knowledge, was the fact that Europe, or the Atlantic region of Europe north of Spain, became incomparably more wealthy than any other part of the world. The new wealth, in the widest sense, meaning conveniences in every form, was produced by the increasing scientific and technical knowledge, which in turn it helped to produce; and the two together, more wealth and more knowledge, helped to form one of the most far-reaching ideas of modern times, the idea of progress.[2]

Palmer points out that the new wealth did not depend on concentrated industry, but 'represented the flowering of the older merchant capitalism, domestic industry and mercantilist government policies'.[3]

Then came the nineteenth century:

> The processes of industrialization in the long run were to revolutionize the lives of men everywhere. In the short run, in the generation following the peace of Vienna, the same processes had pronounced political effects. The Industrial Revolution, by greatly enlarging both the business and the wage-earning classes, doomed all attempts at 'reaction,' attempts, that is, to undo or check the consequences of the French Revolution. Industrialization made the flood of progress too powerful for conservatism to dam up. It hastened the growth of that worldwide economic system whose rise in the eighteenth century has already been observed. And since industrialization first took place in western Europe, one of its early effects

was to widen the difference between eastern and western Europe, and so to weaken the efforts made, after the defeat of Napoleon, to organize a kind of international union of Europe.[4]

This 'industrial revolution', in Palmer's account, centred on the shift to machine production in factories. The combination of industrialization and the French Revolution 'led after 1815 to the proliferation of doctrines and movements of many sorts'.[5] The 'isms' began; European political history took the shapes of liberalism, radicalism, republicanism, socialism, conservatism, nationalism and occasionally humanitarianism. In the west, the bourgeoisie triumphed, and faced a mass of estranged workers.

These changes, according to Palmer, occurred in the context of rapid population growth:

All students agree in attributing the increase to falling death rates rather than to increasing birth rates. Populations grew because more people lived longer, not because more were born. It is probable that a better preservation of civil order reduced death rates in both Asia and Europe. In Europe the organized sovereign states, as established in the seventeenth century, put an end to a long period of civil wars, stopping the chronic violence and marauding, with the accompanying insecurity of agriculture and of family life, which were more deadly than wars fought by armies between governments. . . . In Europe, sooner than in Asia, other causes of growth were at work beyond the maintenance of civil peace. They included the liberation from certain endemic diseases, beginning with the subsiding of bubonic plague in the seventeenth century and the conquest of smallpox in the eighteenth; the improvement of agricultural output, beginning notably in England about 1750; the improvement of transportation, which, by road, canal, and railroad, made localized famine a thing of the past since food could be moved into areas of temporary shortage; and, lastly, the development of machine industry, which allowed large populations to subsist in Europe by trading with peoples overseas.[6]

Thereafter Europeans – the French first of all – began to control births, a small-family system came to prevail and population growth slowed. Fast urbanization and vast emigration complemented the fertility decline. The huge, impersonal, anonymous city epitomized the new society that emerged from the Industrial Revolution.

Palmer's deft summaries of European social history, as understood in 1950, provide us with a baseline for examining what social historians have accomplished since then. A Palmer writing in 1985 would make significant changes: he would acknowledge the contribution of fertility increases to eighteenth-century population growth, stress the proletarianization of the 'peasant' population before 1800; and date a number of changes in family structure well before the industrial concentration and fertility decline of the nineteenth century. He would less confidently assert Europe's eighteenth-century economic superiority to the rest of the world. A 1985 Palmer would reduce the importance of the nineteenth century in the creation of secular proletarian life, and shift emphasis from technological towards organizational change. Social historians have offered major revisions to 1950s knowledge.

Some of the revisions are essentially technical. As a consequence of social-historical research, for example, we now know that European populations recuperated very quickly from the great shocks of mortality occasioned by famine and disease – not to mention that in the great famines after 1500 people rarely starved to death, but instead became more vulnerable to various diseases. Crises accelerated the deaths of the kinds of people who already had relatively high risks of death. In the aftermaths of crises, marriages generally accelerated and fertility rose. The most plausible explanation is that the heightened mortality opened up niches – farms, jobs, household positions – permitting marriage to people who would otherwise have married later, or not at all.

That series of discoveries does not contradict any major understanding of the modern era, but it does give the lie to two common notions: first, that before recent centuries European populations declined or grew mainly as a result of the presence or absence of wars and other demographic disasters; second, that in the absence of crisis European pre-industrial populations were breeding at the limit of their capacity. Thus, a technical revision significantly affects our sense of the misery of social life and limits the explanations we may plausibly offer for popular action or inaction.

Some of the revisions are chiefly factual. Social historians have established, for example, that before 1800 many European villages had rates of population turnover well above 20 per cent per year; rural areas with many wage-labourers had an especially strong tendency to lose residents. The fact contradicts any depiction of 'pre-industrial' populations, especially of rural populations, as stodgily immobile.[7] The finding therefore raises doubts about accounts of nineteenth- and twentieth-century popular political movements as responses to rising mobility and to the breaking up of self-contained, immobile communities. Since such accounts abound, the factual revision makes a difference to historical understanding.

Some recent social history, furthermore, has directly attacked prevailing interpretations of European historical experience. A generation of 'historians from below', for example, have not succeeded in creating a unified popular history. But they have effectively destroyed the old characterization of European workers and peasants as a dumb, slow-moving mass that reacted mainly to extreme hardship and only developed political awareness with the various mobilizations of the nineteenth and twentieth centuries. Social historians have replaced that characterization with a multiplicity of peasants and workers, each group following a relatively well-defined path of changing interests, each acting or failing to act as a function of those changing interests.

In the very process of arguing over the proper distinctions, over the incidence of crucial changes in production and reproduction and over the exact conditions promoting action or inaction, social historians have generally adopted a broadly Marxist conclusion: that changing interests rooted in transformations of production account for major alterations in the collective action of Europe's subordinate classes. Here no single fact or technical discovery is at issue; social history has implanted a new interpretation of a major set of changes.

At the broadest level, European social historians have dislodged two fundamental ideas about European history since 1500: first, the idea of a single sharp break with the traditional past, dividing history into before and after a technologically

49

driven industrial revolution; and second, the idea of a general process, followed in country after country, in which an inexorable logic of differentiation, depending on the expansion of markets and the advance of technical knowledge, impels social evolution – whether 'advance' or 'decline' – and thus poses repeated problems of integration to rapidly changing societies. Those connected ideas, once the chief devices for ordering the recent experiences of the European populace, are the principal casualties of social history's victories.

Increasingly, then, research in social history has forced a recognition of the great mobility of European rural life before 1750; of substantial swings in the rates of birth, death and marriage long before our own time; of extensive rural involvement in regional, national and international markets; of widespread manufacturing and significant proletarianization in the countryside well before the day of factories and steam-power; of struggles between expanding states and populations that fought state-makers' demands for more and more resources; of the rooting of demands for popular sovereignty in resistance to the aggrandizements of states and capitalists.

Another shift in orientation follows from the last few decades' work in European social history: a diminution of the nineteenth century's place as the pivot of modern social change. The move towards implosion[a] and centralization, on the one hand, and the sheer quantity of displacement, on the other, certainly marked off the nineteenth century as a critical period of change. Yet the state-making of the sixteenth and seventeenth centuries, the proletarianization of the seventeenth and eighteenth centuries and the organizational expansion of the twentieth century all rival the nineteenth-century transformations in their impact on routine social life.

The drama of 'before' and 'after' serves poorly as an organizing principle for European social history, whether the pivot is the Industrial Revolution, the onset of modernization or something else. The true problem falls into three parts:

1 specifying the character, timing, and regional incidence of
   (a) the growth of national states, (b) the development of capitalism, (c) the interaction between them (the specification must keep sight of the fact that the phenomena called 'states'

and 'capitalism' themselves altered radically between the six-teenth and twentieth centuries, and that therefore neither the growth of national states nor the development of capital-ism constitutes a unilinear, quantitative progression over the entire period since 1500);

2 tracing through time and space the varying experiences of small social units: individuals, kin groups, households, neighbourhoods, shops, communities and others; and

3 establishing the cause-and-effect connections between the two sets of changes.

That is a large programme.

Before reviewing the facts of nineteenth-century change, let us consider the theoretical problem. Theoretically, what does the three-point programme entail? Capitalism is a system of production in which people who control capital make the basic decisions concerning the productive use of land, labour and capital, and produce by means of labour power bought from workers whose households survive through the sale of labour power. In general terms, the development of capitalism makes three conflicts salient: first, the opposition of capital and labour; second the opposition of capitalists to others who claim control over the same factors of production; and third, market competition: buyers–buyers, buyers–sellers, sellers–sellers. All three conflicts can divide an entire population in two.

The growth of national states means the increasing control of the resources in a relatively large, contiguous territory by an organization that is formally autonomous, differentiated from other organizations, centralized, internally co-ordinated and in possession of major concentrated means of coercion. Like the development of capitalism, state-making follows a triple logic: first, the extraction of resources from the subject population; second, competition between agents of the state and agents of other governments inside and outside the terri-tory; and third, competition among organizations that are sub-ject to the state for resources controlled by the state. Again, all three conflicts can, in principle, produce fundamental div-isions of the entire population.

If capitalism and state-making were to proceed simul-taneously, we might reasonably expect accommodation

51

between capitalists and state-makers. Here is an idealized sequence:

> *early*: capitalist property created as state-makers struggle to extract resources and check rivals; major themes of conflict: expropriation, imposition of state control, imposition of capitalist control and resistance to all of them;
> *late*: with an existing state and established capitalist property, major themes of conflicts: capital–labour opposition, market competition, attempts to control the state and its resources.

These are tendencies. Rather than a rapid transition, we might expect a gradual shift of the bulk of conflicts from type one to type two. In addition, the pattern should depend on the relative rapidity of the two processes; where capitalism comes early and state-making late, for example, we may reasonably expect to find capitalists themselves opposing relatively effective resistance to the state's expansion of its extractive and coercive power. Where state-making leads, in contrast, we are likely to find more intense popular resistance to extraction, if only because capitalists have done less to expropriate and monetize the factors of production.

So, at least, runs the theory. These statements fall far short of a documented historical account. Indeed, they contradict accounts that many people have found plausible – notably the classic nineteenth-century accounts in which rapid social change, driven by differentiation and technical innovation, disrupts stable, immobile societies and thereby promotes disorganization, disorder and protest. My account makes the conflicts that accompany capitalism and state-making intrinsic to their development, consequences of opposing interests built into their very structure.

European social history here sets yet another challenge: to adjudicate between the sort of interest-oriented account of state-making and capitalism I have sketched and classic change–disorder accounts of the same changes.

Nineteenth-century observers who articulated the classic change–disorder accounts were right on one count: great alterations in social life were occurring. Let me offer a rapid summary of the changes brought by the nineteenth century, without guaranteeing that most European social historians would agree with my account.[8]

For several centuries before the nineteenth, industrial expansion occurred mainly in small towns and rural areas. Small capitalists multiplied rapidly. They did not work chiefly as manufacturers in our sense of the word. They operated instead as merchants, giving out work to formally independent groups of workers, most of them organized in households. The social relationships between capitalists and workers ranged from various 'purchase' arrangements in which producers owned the tools, premises, raw materials and finished goods to various 'putting-out' arrangements in which the merchant owned some or all of them; on the whole, the less workers owned, the greater the power of merchants. These systems accumulated capital, but set serious limits on its concentration. The multiplication of semi-independent producers in households and small shops therefore accounted for most of manufacturing's large increase.

Contrary to later prejudices, the European populations involved in these merchant-dominated forms of manufacturing and in commercial agriculture moved a great deal. They moved, however, mainly within regional labour markets or in large systems of circular migration. Both regional labour markets and long-distance circuits left some migrants in cities, but altogether migration, fertility and mortality produced only modest rates of urban growth. Cities increased and lost population largely as a function of levels of activity in their hinterlands.

The nineteenth century changed many of these traits. Capital concentrated. Individual capitalists and organized firms began to control much greater productive means than they had previously commanded. Capitalists seized hold of productive processes. Instead of continuing to organize manufacturing around supplies of self-sustaining labour, they increasingly placed production near markets and sources of energy or raw materials. Production began to edge out exchange as the pivot of capitalist social relationships.

As a result, the active sites of proletarianization shifted from country to city. More and more production went on in large firms employing disciplined wage-earners. Workers migrated from dispersed industrial hamlets, villages and towns.

This urban implosion of capital and labour accelerated rural–urban migration, spurred urban population growth, de-industrialized large sections of the countryside and accentuated differences between town and country; the division between industrial cities and their agricultural hinterlands reappeared with a vengeance. Mechanization of production facilitated the concentration of capital and the subordination of labour.

The coincidence of implosion and mechanization created the illusion of an 'industrial revolution' driven by technological change. Although new technologies certainly contributed to the fixing, disciplining and intensification of labour, much of the nineteenth-century expansion of production preceded the spread of the factory and assembly line, occurred without substantial changes in the actual techniques of production, and depended mainly on alterations in the social relations of production. In textiles, chemicals and metal production, technical innovations promoted dramatic increases in the scale and intensity of production. But for manufacturing in general, two essentially social innovations played a larger part in transforming production: first, the grouping of workers in large shops under centralized time-discipline; and second, the monopolization of means of production by capitalists.

At the start of the nineteenth century, many capitalists worked essentially as merchants, buying and selling the products of workers. No need to exaggerate: in some branches of textiles and metals, full-fledged industrial capitalists ran large mills and employed full-time wage-workers. In cottage industry, merchants often owned the looms and the raw materials worked by poor cottagers. In capitalized segments of European agriculture, the daily or yearly wage already provided the principal income of millions of households. Nevertheless, relatively few capitalists knew how to produce the goods they sold, and many workers did. During the nineteenth century, in industry after industry, capitalists and workers struggled over knowledge and control of detailed production decisions. By the end of the nineteenth century, many capitalists knew how to make a whole product, and few workers did. The capitalists had won.

Workers, however, received some consolation prizes. Towards the end of the nineteenth century – with great variation by region and trade – workers' real income began to rise, and some workers even began to accumulate wealth in the form of housing and household goods. An illusory *embourgeoisement* occurred: in material possessions, leisure and personal style the apparent differences between bourgeois and proletarians diminished, as workers' control of productive capital continued to decline. To some extent, workers' organizations gained legal standing, financial strength and the right to bargain with capitalists. Thus workers acquired a stake in the capitalist system while losing control of the means of production.

As capitalism entered a new phase of concentration and control, European *states* were also undergoing great alterations.[9] By the later eighteenth century, zealous princes, ministers and generals had made national states the dominant organizations in most parts of Europe. The chief exceptions were the urban-commercial band extending from northern Italy across the Alps, down the Rhine and into the Low Countries, and the south-eastern flank of the continent, along which tribute-taking empires, powerful lineages and Islamic peoples concentrated.

Where national states held sway, preparations for war became extensive and costly; military expenditure and payment for war debts occupied the largest shares of most state budgets. The strongest states built great structures for the extraction of the means of war: supplies, food, conscripts and money.

Paradoxically, the very construction of large military organizations reduced the autonomy of military men and created large civilian bureaucracies. The process of bargaining with ordinary people for their acquiescence and their surrender of resources engaged the civilian managers of states willy-nilly in establishing perimeters to state control, limits to state violence and regular routines for eliciting the consent of the subject population. In sixteenth-century England, Tudor monarchs succeeded in disbanding their great lords' private armies, in snatching most fortresses from private hands and in radically reducing the settlement of disputes among nobles by force of arms. Yet even the seizure of property from churches and rebellious lords did not free Tudor monarchs from financial dependence on parliament. Eventually, the consent of parliament became essential to royal war-making, and thus to state expansion itself.

The bargaining process had a different history in each state. But overall it led to the state's civilianization, and to the establishment of regular mechanisms for consulting representatives of the governed population.

Up to the nineteenth century, European states continued to rule indirectly. For routine enforcement of their decisions, collection of revenues and maintenance of public order, they relied chiefly on local powerholders. The powerholders did not derive their tenure or their power from the good will of superiors in a governmental hierarchy. They retained room for manoeuvre on behalf of their own interests. Much of the work of national authorities therefore consisted of negotiating with regional and local powerholders. Ordinary people carried on active political lives, but almost exclusively on a regional or local level. When they did involve themselves in national power struggles, they ordinarily did so through the mediation of local powerholders, or in alliance with them.

In the nineteenth century, this system disappeared from much of Europe. War kept getting more expensive and deadly, but it increasingly involved conquest outside of Europe rather than struggles among European powers. Revolutionary and reformist governments extended direct rule into local communities. The French revolutionaries of 1789 and thereafter were the first Europeans to succeed in that effort at the scale of a large state; revolutionary committees, revolutionary militias and eventually a revolutionary bureaucracy brought individual citizens face to face with the national state. The Napoleonic Empire solidified these revolutionary practices. The French Revolution was precocious and unique. But most European states soon underwent their own transitions to direct rule – many of them, in fact, as a result of conquest by French armies.

As they bargained with local people for even greater resources, state-makers solidified representative institutions, binding national elections and a number of other means by which local people participated regularly in national politics. Here the variation ran even wider than in the institution of direct rule. At the end of the nineteenth century, the Swiss federation, the British parliamentary system, the Italian state (formally very centralized, informally very fragmented) and the bureaucratized Russian Empire represented very different alternatives.

Under pressure from their constituents, managers of most states took on responsibilities for public services, economic infrastructure and household welfare to degrees never previously attained. On the whole, they also moved from reactive to active repression: from violent reactions against rebellion and resistance after they occurred towards active surveillance of the population and towards vigorous efforts to forestall rebellion and resistance. These activities shoved aside autonomous local or regional powerholders, and put functionaries in their places. As a consequence, powerholders lost much of their strength and attractiveness as intermediaries in the attempts of ordinary people to realize their interests. Those were the nineteenth century's great changes.

Or so it seems to me. It is only fair to warn that my synthesis remains unproven and contestable in a number of regards. Consider, for example, the question of mobility and connectedness before and after the nineteenth century. When Eugen Weber seeks to determine how France's multiple peasantries coalesced into a common Frenchness during the nineteenth century, he fixes on awareness of nationality, involvement in national politics and responsiveness to opportunities outside the locality as the phenomena to be explained. Weber lays out the materials of folklorists and travellers brilliantly; he shows us a nineteenth-century rural France fragmented in language and custom, then much stirred by the arrival of the railroad, of obligatory primary education, of widespread military service. 'Between 1880 and 1910', concludes Weber,

> fundamental changes took place on at least three fronts. Roads and railroads brought hitherto remote and inaccessible regions into early contact with the markets and lifeways of the modern world. Schooling taught hitherto indifferent millions the language of the dominant culture, and its values as well, among them patriotism. And military service drove those lessons home.[10]

In Weber's view a congeries of immobile rural societies broke open, connected and began to move.

Yet Weber's basic argument is not convincing. It is debatable

57

how much more intensely French rural people of 1900 were involved in national affairs than were their ancestors of 1800. The vast systems of temporary migration portrayed by Alain Corbin, Abel Châtelain and Abel Poitrineau, for example, established intense ties between alpine villages and Marseille, between impoverished farms of the Limousin and central Paris.[11] Those systems thrived in the eighteenth century, and atrophied in the nineteenth. In certain respects, the integration between those distant rural places and the rest of France actually declined. That is one of my reasons for doubting the classic account of mobilization, even when presented with the richness and subtlety of Weber's analysis. But the presence of Weber's analysis and the credence many historians have given it testify that my alternative account is not self-evident.

Or take the extent of proletarianization before the nineteenth century. The evidence on European people's – and especially whole households' – employment throughout the year is quite fragmentary. It could turn out that the majority of people who worked in cottage industry before 1800 actually spent so much of their years (or their lives) cultivating their own land that the term 'proletarian' describes them badly.

A lot depends, in any case, on how stringent a definition of 'proletarian' we adopt. If, for instance, we insist on full-time wage-earners holding closely supervised positions within large organizations, wage-earners who have no other employment, then proletarianization concentrates by definition in the nineteenth and twentieth centuries.

The effect of minimizing employment in cottage industry before 1800 and adopting a very demanding definition of 'proletarian' is to maintain my statements about trends but to displace the bulk of European proletarianization into the nineteenth and twentieth centuries. (In that case, we must invent a new terminology to designate the millions of European households *before* the nineteenth century, in manufacturing and agriculture alike, that came to depend for survival on wage-labour under capitalist supervision, but did not work in large firms under time-discipline, and so on). The same sort of debate – partly factual, partly definitional – can easily arise about other elements of my summary. The general trends, nevertheless, now seem well established.

CONCLUSION

Not that social history has settled everything. Far from it! In challenging old ideas of popular involvement in big structural changes, European social historians have renewed and displaced the debate, but have by no means ended it. These days social historians of Europe are disagreeing about whether a modern, affectionate, egalitarian family formed, and if so how, when and why. They are worrying about the conditions, if any, under which social classes defined by the relations of production became significant actors. They are pitting against each other alternative explanations of the general European decline in fertility. They are considering the virtues and vices of oral history, of ethnographic approaches to historical analysis, of quantification, of narrative, of most of the procedures I have described as accomplishments of social history. In very recent years, it has become much clearer that social–scientific interventions in social history, where successful, have served mainly to specify what is to be explained and to eliminate bad explanations rather than to supply new and more convincing explanations; that realization has come as a disappointment to historians who hoped for closure. In all these regards, and more, European social history remains a rough, contested terrain.

Yet European social history has much to celebrate. First, it has shown the way to renew our understanding of collective historical experience by systematic collation of many, many individual experiences; historical demography provides a dramatic example of renewed understanding through collective biography. Second, European social history has humanized and historicized those rather abstract and timeless social sciences that have come into its scope; sociology, political science and even economics have emerged more historical from their encounter with European social history. Third, the practitioners of European social history have radically reduced the plausibility of general histories portraying ordinary people as apathetic, irrational or stupid masses. Finally – and most important – European social history has built new accounts of the development of capitalism and the formation of national states, accounts that treat capitalism and states as concrete daily realities rather than vast abstractions, accounts in which the experiences and actions of ordinary people stand in centre stage.

EDITOR'S NOTE

a Tilly uses this term to denote the concentration of capital and labour, as when a cotton mill replaces many dispersed looms.

NOTES

Reprinted from Olivier Zunz (ed.) *Reliving the Past: The Worlds of Social History* (Chapel Hill, NC, 1985). Copyright © 1985, The University of North Carolina Press. Used by permission of the author and publisher.

1 Robert R. Palmer, *A History of the Modern World* (New York, 1950).
2 ibid: 264–5.
3 ibid: 264.
4 ibid: 432.
5 ibid: 441.
6 ibid: 569.
7 For example, Sune Åkerman, Hans Christian Johansen and David Gaunt (eds), *Chance and Change: Social and Economic Studies in Historical Demography in the Baltic Area* (Odense, 1978); Ingrid Eriksson and John Rogers, *Rural Labor and Population Change: Social and Demographic Development in East-Central Sweden during the Nineteenth Century* (Stockholm, 1978); Sture Martinius, *Befolkningsrörlighet under industrialismens inledningsskede i Sverige* (Gothenberg, 1967); John Pattern, *Rural–Urban Migration in Pre-Industrial England* (Oxford, 1973) School of Geography, Occasional Papers, 6.
8 In ideas, sources and text, this section draws heavily on Charles Tilly, *Big Structures, Large Processes, Huge Comparisons* (New York, 1985).
9 For background, see Charles Tilly (ed.), *The Formation of National States in Western Europe* (Princeton, NJ, 1975).
10 Eugen Weber, *Peasants into Frenchmen. The Modernization of Rural France* (Stanford, Calif., 1976): 493–4. For a critique of Weber, see Charles Tilly, 'Did the cake of custom break?', in John M. Merriman (ed.), *Consciousness and Class Experience in Nineteenth-Century Europe,* (New York, 1979): 17–44.
11 Alain Corbin, *Archaisme et modernité en Limousin au XIXe siècle* (Paris, 1975); Abel Châtelain, *Les migrants temporaires en France de 1800 à 1914,* 2 vols (Villeneuve d'Ascq, 1976); Abel Poitrineau, *Remues d'hommes. Les migrations montagnardes en France, XVIIe-XVIIIe siècles* (Paris, 1983).

Part II

WORK EXPERIENCES AND PROTEST

Charles Tilly has characterized social history as studying how ordinary people lived 'the big events'. Much historical research since 1960 has been preoccupied with that question. How did ordinary people, especially wage-earners, live the changes in production methods of the last two centuries? The drama inherent in the question concerns how workers with traditional habits and expectations confronted the changes that commercial and industrial capitalism imposed on them. We have begun to see the inadequacies of the concept of the Industrial Revolution to capture many aspects of this experience. Theresa McBride's essay reinforces this point by exploring women workers. Christopher Johnson shows why it is mistaken to think of mechanization as the moving force for social and political change. Finally, James Roberts takes the reader into nineteenth-century factories and examines the quality of discipline.

4

WOMEN'S WORK AND INDUSTRIALIZATION

Theresa McBride

Women's presence in the workplace, so often portrayed as a novelty today, actually has deep historical roots. And if historians are to give ordinary people their place in history, then the history of women workers is an important part of the agenda. The growth of women's movements and dramatic changes in family life today draw still more attention to the question of how women lived the great events.

It is not the case that studies of the Industrial Revolution totally ignore women workers. Textbooks frequently note that young women were an important source of labour in the new textile mills of the late eighteenth and nineteenth centuries. The mill girls' drudgery, often for 13 or 14 hours a day, has been denounced many times.

These observations are a start, but they hardly fulfil the quest to learn how women experienced the great socio-economic changes of the past few centuries. Theresa McBride's magisterial survey of this issue questions whether the Industrial Revolution is a key to understanding the fate of female wage-earners. Her analysis takes the reader far afield from factories and machine production.

Readers would do well to ask whether the history of women's work fits neatly into the categories developed to describe the history of men's work. This task includes examining the notions that Tilly and Samuel (and in the next essay, Johnson) have put forward as an alternative to the Industrial Revolution.

* * *

Industrialization is an irreversible and seemingly inevitable process. Whether beneficial or disastrous, the changes wrought by industrialization represent the most profound changes in

63

the nature of daily life since the establishment of stable agricultural societies. Yet the ordinary people most affected by industrialization have left few records of their reactions and, consequently, there remain many unanswered questions about its effects. In particular, one group that has been little considered in the written histories of industrialization until very recently is women. In spite of some historians' assumption that to write about the history of men includes the history of women, women experience historical processes differently. Women differ from men both biologically and in the roles they have played throughout history; industrialization affected them uniquely, just as their participation in the industrial process was distinctive. Hence, this chapter consists of an explanation of women's special roles during this period and encompasses an examination of a wide variety of women's experiences during industrialization.

Since industrialization consisted most basically of a change in the structure of work, the first questions we will attempt to answer relate to women as workers: the types of work they performed, their attitudes towards work and their participation in industrial protests. Second, we must examine the female role in a more general context. How did industrialization alter women's status and function in the family structure? Finally, we must evaluate the advantages and disadvantages of industrialization as women experienced them, as workers, as wives, as mothers.

Women have always worked. The Industrial Revolution did not usher in a new phase in the employment of women in that sense. But the nineteenth century did 'discover' the woman worker as an object of pity, and the Victorian social conscience was aroused as never before by the plight of working women and children.[1] Because women's work in the pre-industrial world had been home-based and largely seasonal, work had not seriously interfered with women's responsibilities in child care and household duties. But industrialization required that workers perform their jobs away from their homes, and the industrial process could not tolerate an erratic workforce. Thus, industrialization exacerbated the problems of a working mother and made her plight more visible, even though the fact of her work was scarcely new.

The crucial factor in woman's work experience involves her duality of roles. In addition to her primary biological and social role as wife and mother, the women in pre-industrial and early industrial societies made a vital contribution to the family's total earnings. In the nineteenth century, as a general estimate, more than two-thirds of all single women worked and between one-quarter and one-half of married women were employed, depending on the geographical area. Most women worked for several years before marriage, which occurred for the average western European woman at about the age of 24.[2] The average female life-cycle then included a long period of childbearing and childrearing, generally shortened only by sterility or by death. Most women worked sporadically during this period in agriculture or in the various kinds of domestic manufacturing. But industrialization introduced a conflict between the two female roles by separating the place of work from the home, and thus initiated the eventual decline of women's work opportunities and the virtual disappearance of married women from the workforce until the very recent past.[3]

Women in the pre-industrial era were mainly employed in agriculture, domestic manufacturing and household service. Pre-industrial society also emphasized the 'family economy', i.e., the determination of family subsistence by the contributions of all family members capable of earning. Paradoxically, women were often underemployed because of their extensive familial obligations, which caused them to work only sporadically or seasonally and close to home.

Industrialization affected women most profoundly through the separation of work and home. Facing a conflict between their family obligations and their ability to earn money, women ultimately altered their occupational choices, experienced a fundamental reformulation of their attitudes about work and gradually developed a characteristically female work pattern. This evolution of the structure of women's work and feminine attitudes about work can be divided into three phases. The first phase from the 1760s to about 1880; the second from the 1880s through the 1940s; and the third, the post-war period. This division of the process into phases should not be interpreted to mean that women's employment underwent a radical change in the 1880s or again in the 1940s. One could view the whole of phases one and two as a unified period of gradual adjustment to industrialization. Indeed, it is not the particular years that are important in this process but the stages of development, which must be adjusted to fit different national patterns.[4] This essay will concentrate almost exclusively upon phase one with some analysis of the transition to phase two, but it is important to understand how these two phases contributed to permanent changes in women's working lives.

The first phase consisted of the persistence of artisanal production, of the expansion of domestic manufacturing (piecework done by workers in their own homes) and of the rapid development of the textile industry, particularly the cotton industry. This first phase was a transitional period of employment for both single and married women in domestic production and the early textile mills, in domestic service and agriculture. But in the long run, women's employment opportunities began to decline and become associated with the stagnating textile industry, along with domestic manufacturing, agriculture and domestic service, which had all begun to contract by phase two. In the second phase, from the 1880s until after the Second World War, the structure of industry changed towards heavy industries like mining, metallurgy and machines, and this meant a significant decrease in married women's work.

Indeed, the most significant change in women's work to emerge from industrialization was the notion that women should retire from work when they married. This idea arose partially from the assumption that the male wage alone should be sufficient to support a family. But it also reflected a kind of resolution of the conflict introduced by industrialization between the married woman's two roles since, in effect, it reduced her to a single primary role. Combined with some redistribution of the female workforce, this decline in married women's work and the contingent pattern of a merely temporary work experience represented the most typical aspect of phase two.

The third and contemporary phase constitutes the eventual outcome of this long process of adjustment and marks a radical break with pre-industrial and early industrial work patterns for both married and single women. Only in the recent past have women begun to re-enter the labour force in a diversity of occupations and in significant numbers with the prospect that this may signify a permanent trend.[5] How soon this may result in a change of attitudes about the permanency of work in the female life-cycle or about the kinds of jobs preferred by women we cannot yet predict.

Historians often search for the most pervasive changes in lifestyles in the sectors of the economy that were modernizing rapidly during industrialization, but this search will be fruitless for those interested in the ways in which most women experienced industrialization. Most women in the early industrial period continued to be employed in their traditional occupations: in agriculture, in domestic service, in domestic manufacturing and in commercial distribution. In England, more rapid urbanization and the decline of agriculture forced some women into new roles much earlier – by the middle of the nineteenth century. But in France and throughout Europe, agriculture remained the most important employer of women until the post–1880 period, and women clung to other traditional occupations like domestic service until late in the century.[6]

Additionally, the continental countries preserved the tradition of employing women in domestic manufacturing much longer because the home workers were not so heavily concentrated in cotton-cloth production, which declined early in the nineteenth century leaving many British home workers unemployed. But even in England, the factories absorbed only a minority of women in the nineteenth century. In England in 1841 female factory operatives numbered only 8,879.[7] Obviously, this was not the typical form of female employment. Thus, while one often cites the English example as the key to industrialization, the French experience was more typical of the evolution of female work roles in the west.

Women's employment in the first phase of industrialization continued to be concentrated in four major categories: agriculture, domestic manufacturing, retail distribution and domestic service. In France in 1866 nearly 2 million women were still employed in agriculture, compared with about 1 million in all aspects of manufacturing (both factory work and domestic production).[8] Female employment in agriculture remained high throughout Europe wherever the pattern of small farms was customary, but women also were increasingly employed as day-labourers in large-scale agriculture, particularly in the expanding wine industry and in the growing of beets for sugar and alcohol. Women involved in wine-growing participated in a culture that was almost urban, for the wine-growers lived in large villages and their lives were influenced by the market economy much more than the average peasant's.[9] Large-scale agriculture thus involved women in a partly urban and modernized culture. Though a traditional occupation for women, agriculture thus remained a significant employment option that could provide women with experiences that had considerable consequences for their modernization.

Wine-growing was one method of supplementing the average income of an agricultural family, but domestic manufacturing was another. When wine-growing proved unprofitable, or in those areas that could not accommodate viniculture, the women turned to lace-making or spinning or silk-weaving. Throughout the early industrial period, women workers dominated the domestic labour force; they represented three-quarters of this group in France in 1866. Like the pre-industrial textile family, the early industrial family was an economic unit. The father worked as a weaver (work considered too difficult and too dangerous for a woman) and apprenticed his older sons to his trade, while the mother, assisted by younger children, did the spinning, combing and carding. In the early textile mills in England, this configuration remained relatively unchanged at first, since the family could be hired to work as a team in the factory.[10] Or, as a variation of this arrangement, the father and sons would be hired as weavers to work in the mill, while the mother and daughters continued to work at spinning in their cottages. In this way, both domestic production and factory work expanded during the first phase of industrialization.

The textile industry provides us with a classic example of the way in which industrialization disproportionately and temporarily increased certain jobs that became almost exclusively female. Even though most women were employed elsewhere, female labour was vital to the early factories, where women and children constituted 40 per cent of the total labour force. Women were paid about half as much as adult male workers, so that single women who were helping to support their families or women whose husbands also worked in the factories were the most likely to take up this kind of work. But women benefited both from the proliferation of the factories and the rising level of domestic manufacturing.

Since domestic manufacturing was scarcely new to women, and factory work involved only a small minority, many of the traditional aspects of women's work experience persisted. Industrialization did not immediately disrupt the pattern of the family working together as a unit of production. Clearly, the family economy, to which all members contributed their earnings, remained as strong as ever, and women, whether as wives or daughters, continued to assume a major part of the family's economic responsibilities.[11]

But it would be inaccurate to overemphasize the traditionalism that this kind of work perpetuated. Both the single and the married women employed in textile production were exposed to novel circumstances and experiences. Increasing contacts with intermediaries and with the market must have enhanced their market sense. Because they could contribute on a more regular basis to the family income, they often gained more status in family decisions. Women had always played an important role in western European families by managing the family budget, and their economic decisions assumed greater importance as the family's income rose above the level of subsistence.[12] It was women's desires for small consumer goods like metal pins and buttons that expanded the domestic market for such products and in turn created more work for the women who produced them.[13] Thus, new experiences and new attitudes emerged within the context of traditional roles and occupations.

While single women in this period could seek work as domestic servants and in the factories, married women tended to be employed in agriculture, domestic manufacturing or in part-time or casual employment often associated with retailing. Married women commonly worked in food shops or beer houses or bars or helped to run small shops or inns. In the industrialized area of Lancashire, in the mid-nineteenth century 26 per cent of the wives living with their husbands were recorded in the census as gainfully employed on a regular basis.[14] About one-third of these worked in the non-factory occupations described here. Those who were employed, particularly in the factories, were primarily the youngest wives, who had few or no children to care for. Many other wives, who were not recorded in the census as employed, supplemented the family income by taking in lodgers or doing some cleaning part time or taking in laundry. Thus, retailing occupations and other service jobs remained a consistent employment option for married women throughout phase one.

But the largest employer of women in the nineteenth century, and the dominant employment option for single women after agriculture, was domestic service. In the nineteenth century, domestic service employed more women than all types of manufacturing put together.[15] The size of the domestic servant class rose rapidly in phase one, then remained stable during phase two and declined in total numbers only at the end of phase two during the Second World War. During the first phase of industrialization, about one in every three women in Europe was a servant at some time in her life.

Domestic service comprised an amorphous occupational group in the nineteenth century; it included workers as diverse as some dairymaids and some silk-weavers, for the crucial distinction was not the kind of work performed but rather the fact that the worker lived in her employer's household and received her board as compensation for her labour. In the countryside, daughters of tenant farmers traditionally took up employment as servants in neighbouring farms. With industrialization, positions in household service multiplied as the urban middle classes grew in numbers and wealth.

Domestic service in the industrial age frequently involved long-distance migration in search of positions in the cities. In spite of the traditional interpretation of labour migration, which assumed that women tended to travel much shorter distances than men in search of work, domestics' migration was uniquely adventurous.[16] Female domestic servants were considerably more mobile than either females who went to work in factories or males in general. Most servants in the nineteenth century came from rural backgrounds, but few worked in the same areas in which they had been born. Consequently, even though domestic service was a traditional occupation for women, it increased the potential for the weakening of family ties and for the diluting of time-honoured values.

The highly traditional character of domestic service and the accessibility of positions in service explain much of the popularity of household service. But service also offered some distinct advantages over other kinds of work. Domestic service preserved the familial context of work even though it took the young woman out of her own home. The young woman left parental control and protection only to become subordinated to an employer. In fact, the contract for a young servant's services could be arranged between her parents and her employer without her participation, though older, more experienced servants generally found their positions on their own. In spite of low monetary wages, servants were better off than other kinds of workers because of the compensation of room and board. And their contacts with wealthy middle- and upper-class families were often lucrative for loyal servants: Juliette Sauget's memoirs of service in the period just before the First World War recall an employer who wanted to send her to cooking school so that she could qualify for a better job. An occasional servant even received an annual income for life by the death bequest of a grateful employer.

Servants had a reputation for saving, and they constituted the overwhelming majority of depositors in nineteenth-century savings banks. Servants also frequently retained close links with the families they had left behind in the countryside. Many a servant sent all or part of her wages to her parents, suggesting that many young women continued to think of the family as an economic unit. But more individualistic motivations were also evident as servants accumulated dowries so that they could enhance their marriage prospects or sought to use their savings to start a career, for example through apprenticeship to a dressmaker. Gradually, but almost visibly, young women's aspirations became less family oriented.

Though it constituted no clear break with tradition, domestic service involved several new features in the period of early industrialization. Household service became more highly urbanized than ever before. It no longer consisted simply of sending one's daughter to work in a wealthier peasant's house or in the home of the local gentry. As young women moved farther from their parental homes, family ties weakened. Daughters living away from their parents, for example, gained considerably more control over the timing of their own marriages and the choice of their spouses.[17] For most servants, their first positions in service represented their initial encounter with the city and with urban life, and thus the experience became a period of acculturation to urban life and to middle-class values.

The experience of servanthood even more than other kinds of work was individualized and defined by the personal relationship of the servant and her employer, but some of its aspects can be generalized. Servanthood was merely a temporary stage in life; no more than one servant in ten remained a servant throughout her life. Once the servant had settled into the city and accumulated some savings, she generally found herself a husband or another job. Servants were nearly always young and single: in England, 40 per cent of the female servants were under 20; in France, 40 per cent under 25. Live-in domestic service almost required celibacy, since the work days were long (16 to 18 hours) and there were few days off to spend with one's family. This experience of servanthood, then, often coincided with an important transition in an individual's life.

Middle-class employers apparently tried to mould their young servants to accept the middle-class values of cleanliness, sobriety, self-discipline and respect for authority. But many despaired of ever accomplishing this task. In the process, however, servants were inevitably exposed to some basic training (servants were more literate on average than the other members of their rural-born cohort) and to the middle-class emphasis on individual mobility through planning, education and saving. Some servants clearly learned their lessons well. But the heavy-handed stress on total obedience and subservience to the employer's whims could also be devastating. Some servants probably internalized the feelings of inferiority.[18] In fact, a substantial segment of the servant class was unable to cope with the demeaning aspects of service and with the liberation from rural constraints. These individuals entered the ranks of the disreputable poor through the birth of an illegitimate child, through involvement in theft or other crimes, or because of drunkenness. In many cases, the employer class was directly involved in the servant's deterioration; one of the most common motivations listed by Parisian prostitutes in the 1830s for taking up their occupation was a prior seduction by their employer. Ex-domestic servants comprised the largest group of prostitutes. Thus, the employer's paternal authority could be used to destroy an individual as well as to shape her character constructively. Much depended upon the individual employer and the particular servant. Some servants, like a kitchenmaid named Jean Rennie, became defiant in the face of an employer's belittling tactics. When Rennie found a coin placed under a rug to test her honesty, she glued the coin to the floor. She was never tested again.

This period of acculturation, then, had divergent impacts on different individuals. The qualities of cleanliness, obedience and diligence were prized in a wife, so domestic service had a traditional reputation as a better preparation for marriage than other kinds of work. The docile servant was expected to make a docile wife. Other servants' aspirations evolved towards more individualistic goals of self-satisfaction and self-improvement. Most servants changed positions as often as every year either to escape an unpleasant job or to improve their prospects or simply to avoid boredom. Because of the enormous demand for domestic labour, this spirit of independence (which the middle class termed disloyalty) was frequently rewarded by an improvement in wages or working conditions.

Most important, women's experience as domestic servants in phase one established two characteristic trends. First, service was viewed as a useful preparation for later life, but required no lifetime commitment. It should be remembered that since women had always worked, the presumption that formal employment should terminate at marriage was novel. The full consequences of this attitude will be examined more completely later, but the link between this new assumption and the experience of servants is pertinent here. Unlike either agriculture or domestic manufacturing, both service and factory work conflicted too strongly with women's responsibilities as mothers to be continued after marriage and the birth of children. Single women predominated in both domestic service and factory work. But servanthood much more than factory work set the tone for women's work patterns in the industrial era simply because servanthood was the most pervasive shared experience of lower-class women in the nineteenth century and far outweighed factory work in its impact upon a wide number of women.

Second, the preference of women for domestic service over

industrial work suggests that women's dispersion throughout the economy had much to do with their own attitudes about work. Women disliked factory work because it was too impersonal and likely to involve them with bad companions. They preferred service because it offered them a substitute home, though many recognized that service positions were more remunerative than other jobs. This desire for a personal relationship with their employers was not new to women, but neither was it a customary response that dwindled in the industrial context. The desire for a personal relationship in work has remained deeply ingrained in women's approach to occupational choice, and this attitude became firmly established in the early industrial period with the concentration of women in service occupations.

Related to women's attitudes about work in the industrial age is the comparatively low level of women's participation in protest. Because work for women comprised only a temporary stage, they did not feel the same stake in improving their economic position by striking as did male workers. The interruption of work and consequent loss of pay might have seemed an unwanted hindrance to their future plans. Thus, women workers had a low incidence of industrial protests on their own behalf. Nevertheless, women were not absent from industrial protest. In an important strike in 1900 in the Breton town of Fougères, the striking shoemakers had the full support of their wives and daughters, who blocked the roads into the town with their bodies to prevent the arrival of strike-breakers and troops.[19] Women often strongly and violently supported male strikers because these protests related to their own welfare as wives and daughters. But this kind of participation and support underlined women's traditional role as consumers rather than breadwinners.

In summary, women's work experience in phase one of industrialization consisted of some persistence of traditional patterns and of considerable change. The expanding sectors of domestic service, domestic manufacturing and even certain types of factory work had all begun to decline by the 1880s, destroying the temporarily advantageous situation of women workers. But phase one did not consist simply of an interim of adjustment; instead, it represented a crucial transition, particularly in the formation of a modern work pattern for women.

The idea of employment as a temporary stage in a woman's life spread. Women began to develop more individualistic aspirations. And women seemed to exercise some occupational choice as the traditional sectors expanded and new possibilities arose. This choice indicated a clear preference for a personal relationship with an employer. The attitudes thus firmly established by the end of phase one set the pattern for women's work in phase two and many of them pervade modern women's feelings about work.

By the beginning of phase two the fundamental attitudes about work had already been formulated, and the redistribution of women throughout the labour force was already well under way. The decay of family-centred agriculture meant the loss of an important source of female employment, particularly for married women, a process that had begun in phase one if not before. More recently, large-scale agriculture, and specifically viniculture, had suffered a profound crisis with the economic depression of the 1870s and a consistent problem (after 1870) of overproduction. Most types of domestic manufacturing were also on the wane by phase two, replaced by mechanized processes. In France, some of the unemployed domestic textile workers found employment as seamstresses because the garment industry retained its small scale and its outwork system until very late. In England, where the decline of both agriculture and domestic manufacturing had been evident much earlier, some of the surplus female labour had been absorbed into domestic service. But by 1880 the domestic servant class had levelled off and began to decline relative to the total labour force.

The decline of domestic service signifies broader attitudinal changes that coincided with the transition from phase one to phase two. The middle-class housewife was no longer so willing or even financially able to invite a stranger into her home to assist in the household work. The middle-class lifestyle, growing ever more inclusive, became increasingly privatized and demanded greater concentration than ever before by the wife and mother on domestic concerns. The sometimes obstreperous, disorderly and disrespectful servant became too much of a burden, and so was dispensed with in the middle-class household. Servants themselves, unwilling to be subject to the capricious demands of employers and to the demeaning requirements of service, sought employment in other sectors, which offered them more freedom. Urbanization and the spread of primary education also undermined the usefulness of domestic service as a rural–urban link, or even as a period of training before marriage.

For single women, phase two meant new opportunities emerging about the turn of the twentieth century, especially in the tertiary (or service) sector. This sector became increasingly feminized as it expanded, providing numerous jobs for single women in clerical work, and as teachers, nurses and retail clerks. These new work options soon became characteristic female occupations, but they did not provide a considerable source of employment for women until the third phase of industrialization. Part of the reason that employment in the clerical and service areas became identified with women lay in the fact that women continued to take jobs that, like domestic service, provided a personal relationship with an employer or at least greater contact with people. This aspect of work remained important to women even after other types of work had been removed from the family context.

The diversification of single women's employment alternatives resulted less from changes in employer policies, feminist agitation or active opposition from male workers in the older industries than from the changing structure and maturation of industry. Agricultural depression and the stagnation of the textile industry, as we have already mentioned, eliminated much of the temporary work married women had performed in or near their homes and caused single women to move into the tertiary sector. The evolution of large retail outlets in phase two further threatened the small retail shops and family-run businesses, curtailing a consistent source of employment for a minority of married women. Hence, the expansion of single women's employment options was inversely proportional to the decline of married women's status in the labour market.

Again, the evolution of domestic service in phase two is suggestive of a more general pattern. The decline in live-in servants that resulted when younger single women took up other kinds of employment made available greater employment for part-time cleaning women. Virtually the only kind of part-time work available to unskilled older women in the post-1880 period was employment as a daily worker or charwoman, and older women eagerly sought out jobs as poorly paid chars.[20] Thus, while single women were very gradually achieving somewhat more independence and even limited professionalism in their employment, married women's work was declining in numbers of women employed and was increasingly confined to the lowest-status, least-skilled and poorest-paid jobs.

In phase two, then, married women faced vastly reduced options. Married women continued, as in phase one, to work during periods of a husband's illness or unemployment or when advancing age curtailed or eliminated the husband's income. These 'critical life situations' were clustered in the decades of the 1870s and 1890s because of a series of economic crises, but they could occur in individual families at any time, particularly as the couple grew older. Married women's work thus became less a natural phase in a woman's life and was dictated increasingly by the adequacy of her husband's income and by the occurrence of family crises. But married women found fewer opportunities to work even when family hardship forced them to do so.

When the evolution of technology and industrial organization limited women's productive role, they also helped to shape the cultural attitudes that would restrict a woman's activities to the home as never before. The industrial period brought a complex change in the attitudes about children that had a profound impact upon the role of women as mothers. Paradoxically, the new importance attached to the role of the mother came at a time when the reduction in family size also lightened the burden of child-rearing. Not only were women bearing fewer children but these children were being taken out of the home much earlier by the spread of public education. Ironically, society ascribed greater importance to the role of the mother precisely at a time when her function was being undermined or at least significantly altered by the evolution of social institutions.

The impact of industrialization has involved a three-stage process in which the third stage is only beginning. The first stage represented a century-long transition, characterized by a merely temporary increase in women's employment levels and limited reassignment of women in the labour force. But in this first phase, the young women who went to work as domestic servants or factory workers or did piecework at home acquired a particular set of attitudes about work. The modern and typically female work pattern of a short period of employment before marriage reinforced the general attitude that women should not work after marriage but should confine their activities to their maternal responsibilities. Women exercised their preference for social contact or a personal quality in their jobs and consistently entered occupations as facilitators or providers of services. Phase two had little effect on the attitudes already set in phase one, but the maturation of industry channelled many more single women into the modernizing sectors as traditional occupations declined. The major impact of phase two was the irreconcilable polarization of the dual functions of women, confining women to a limited and decidedly inferior position in the workforce.

It is clear in retrospect that women's decline in the labour force during industrialization was merely a temporary phase. Indeed, although phase three lies outside the limits of this essay, current trends suggest that much more permanent and revolutionary changes are now under way in women's employment options and the female commitment to work. Women's return 'home' during industrialization is ending as women and men set off on another road towards an undetermined goal.

NOTES

1 Wanda F. Neff, *Victorian Working Women* (London, 1929): 1.

2 J. Hajnal 'European marriage patterns in perspective', in D. V. Glass and D. E. C. Eversley (eds), *Population in History* (London, 1965): 101–43.

3 Alice Clark, *The Working Life of Women in the Seventeenth Century* (London, 1919), dates the decline in married women's work from a much earlier period. Leonore Davidoff, 'The employment of married women in England, 1850–1950', MA thesis (University of London, 1955–6); Margaret Hewitt, *Wives and Mothers in Victorian Industry* (London, 1958).

4 Eric Richards, 'Women in the British economy since about 1700:

an Interpretation', *History*, LIX (October 1974): 337–57, provides a conceptualization from the English perspective.

5 See, for example, Catherine Bodard Silver, 'Salon, foyer, bureau: women and the professions in France', in Lois Banner and Mary Hartman (eds), *Clio's Consciousness Raised* (New York, 1974): 72–85; and Neal A. Ferguson, 'Women's work: employment opportunities and economic roles, 1918–1939', *Albion*, VII (spring 1975): 55–68.

6 Patricia Branca, 'A new perspective on women's work: a comparative typology', *Journal of Social History*, IX (December 1975), presents an important new conceptualization of women's work history with a European focus.

7 *Census of England and Wales*, 1841.

8 *Statistique générale de la France*, 1866.

9 Theodore Zeldin, *France, 1848–1945*, 2 vols, *Ambition, Love, and Politics* (Oxford, 1973) 1: 165.

10 Neil Smelser, *Social Change in the Industrial Revolution* (London, 1960): esp. 225–64.

11 Joan Scott and Louise Tilly, 'Women's work and the family in nineteenth-century Europe', *Comparative Studies in Society and History*, XVII (1975), argue that women's work experience reflects more traditionalism than change.

12 But this pattern of increased responsibility in determining the family budget may not be true in phase two, when working men tended to keep a larger proportion of their wages before turning over household money to their wives. See Peter N. Stearns, 'Working class women in Britain, 1890–1914', in Martha Vicinus (ed.), *Suffer and Be Still* (Bloomington, Indiana, 1972): 100–20.

13 Neil McKendrick, 'Home demand and economic growth: a new view of the role of women and children in the Industrial Revolution', in Neil McKendrick (ed.) *Historical Perspectives: Studies in English Thought and Society in Honor of J. H. Plumb* (London, 1974): 152–210.

14 Michael Anderson, *Family Structure in Nineteenth-Century Lancashire* (Cambridge, 1971): 71.

15 For a much fuller discussion of domestic service in the nineteenth century, see Theresa M. McBride, *The Domestic Revolution: The Modernization of Household Service in England and France, 1820–1920* (London, 1976).

16 The classic interpretation of labour migration is that of Arthur Redford, *Labor Migration in England, 1800–1850*, rev. edn (New York, 1968): see 183.

17 The research of Vivien Elliott, Research Fellow, Radcliffe Institute, on earlier marriage patterns in England suggests that the important variable in determining how much freedom women had in choosing their own spouses was whether or not they lived at home with their fathers, for this determined how much paternal authority was exercised.

18 Leonore Davidoff, 'Mastered for life: servant and wife in Victorian

and Edwardian England', *Journal of Social History*, VII (June 1974): 406–28.

19 This incident is taken from the research of Allan Binstock, 'The shoemakers of Fougères', Ph.D dissertation (University of Wisconsin, 1975).

20 F. Zweig, *Women's Life and Labour* (London, 1952): 140; see also McBride, *Domestic Revolution*.

5

PATTERNS OF PROLETARIANIZATION

Christopher H. Johnson

When the nineteenth century began, wage-earners everywhere had difficult lives. They struggled, at best, to make ends meet. Poverty accompanied powerlessness. And even as middle-class males began to receive voting rights, workers still had no officially recognized means for participating in politics. None the less, labourers came to demand greater power and more economic justice. They increasingly identified themselves as part of a 'working class' – a term which hardly existed before 1830 – and eventually built powerful protest movements around that identity.

One of the central ambitions of the new labour history has been to connect changes in work conditions with working-class protest and organization. The Marxian assumption that factory labourers would form the insurrectionary proletariat had a certain logic, but detailed investigation into the personnel of labour movements did not bear out the expectation. Rather, handicraft workers, who were furthest from factory conditions, created, led and supported working-class protest. A socialist during the Revolution of 1848 or a trade union leader of 1890 was far more likely to be a tailor than a factory hand.

Christopher Johnson has made major contributions to labour history by explaining the class militancy on the part of craft workers. Johnson's explanation draws upon the proletarianization process. Readers will detect that he uses the terms in a slightly different way from Tilly. Proletarianization for Johnson involves the artisans' loss of control over their work, usually through a degradation of the skills needed on the job. He goes on to make the important point that mechanization did not generally mark the fundamental break in the history of a trade. Factory methods of production usually arrived after workers had already been proletarianized and also radicalized politically.

Labour historians have been very receptive to the proletarianization model as an explanation for class conflict – despite the qualifications with which Johnson ends his essay. It has become, in many ways, the successor to the paradigm of an industrial revolution.

* * *

. . . Few would maintain today that proletarianization has been merely a function of technological development. The imposition of the division and specialization of labour, the wrenching of control over the means and, indeed, the knowledge of production, the disciplining of the labour force and the creation of replaceable labour units: such capitalist strategies predate the rise of modern industrial technology and prepare the way for it. It is not absurd to argue, in fact, that machine production, the factory system, Taylorism[a] and the assembly line must be viewed as much as elements in the further disciplining and controlling of the labour force as devices to achieve greater technical efficiency. . . . [1]

The case studies that have occupied my research interests for several years concern two patterns of proletarianization during this transitional phase. The first fixes upon the path of large-city artisans as structural change engulfs their handicraft industries, the second upon small mono-industrial[b] towns whose industrial character was set well before the machine revolution. In my earlier work on the appeal of radical ideas among French working people and on the incidence of militance expressed through strike activity and socio-political protest, I was consistently struck by the fact that, along with large-city artisans, the worker populations of old, small, industrial cities known for a particular kind of manufactured product, crop up again and again: places in France like Vienne, Reims, Niort, Rive-de-Gier, Elbeuf, Mirecourt, Troyes and Lodève, as well as its nearby sister cities in woollens, Clermond l'Hérault and Bédarieux.[2] For such cities as for the large-city artisans, the Revolution of 1848 was more an end of an era than a beginning. Thereafter, the focus of industrialization, proletarianization and militance tends to shift to the industrial *villes-champignons,*[c] such as the Lille-Roubaix-Tourcoing complex or Clermond-Ferrand and to thriving port cities such as Marseille or Le Havre. Paris and Lyon, of course, hardly fade from the scene, and their proletarianized artisans continue to play a leading role in the working-class movement, but they increasingly share the stage with workers, especially skilled workers, from the 'modern' sector.

Thus the scene is France, 1750 to 1850, the problem urban proletarianization, and the examples a single Parisian craft, tailoring for men, and an old, small, essentially mono-industrial manufacturing town, Lodève.

Journeyman tailors stood at the forefront of the Parisian class struggle during the 1830s and 1840s.[3] Their craft union organization became a model for others, they initiated the great strike of 1840 that included dozens of other trades, they flocked to radical political movements of all sorts and, above all, they pioneered the development of producers' associations, especially through their highly successful co-operative set up in 1848 in the former debtors' prison of Clichy. The search for the causes of such behaviour led me to the careful study of the changing structure of the tailoring industry during the first half of the century. What had occurred was the full swing from a corporative, or guild, mode of production to an industrial capitalist one over the fifty years after the French Revolution. And this change had unfolded without the least mechanization of the industry. Two broad stages in the process can be identified. The first involved personnel within the old corporate structure[d] of pre-revolutionary France as larger master tailors expanded their operations in two basic ways. First, they began to maintain large stocks of cloth and developed elaborate credit arrangements with their suppliers, the cloth merchants. Second, they profoundly altered the relations of production by increasing the size of their workforce, dividing specific tasks according to a hierarchy of skills and, most ominous of all, by hiring unapprenticed home workers, largely women, to sew simpler garments, such as trousers and vests, at half the wage of a journeyman. In the shops of these merchant tailors, as they came to be called, the live-in journeyman became a thing of the past. The abolition of the guilds during the revolution, of course, had been the fundamental legal base for this development. By the mid-1820s, out of approximately 1,800 tailoring shops operating in Paris, perhaps 200 were run by merchant tailors. But most of the smaller traditional masters were also prospering due to lower costs of cloth, Paris's growing population of middle-income people and her reputation that attracted flocks of provincial and foreign bourgeois to her shops. Journeymen also benefited: real wages rose an estimated 15 per cent from 1800 to 1825. In short, tailoring experienced a 'golden age' in the first twenty-five years of the nineteenth century. But storm clouds were beginning to gather.

The industry became overcrowded, and with the depression of the late 1820s, the scene was set for the second stage in the structural change that transformed Parisian tailoring for men. This was the rise of *confection*, ready-made clothing produced in standardized sizes and marketed through department stores. Here the thrust came from outside the craft as large cloth merchants brought their capital, market connections and entrepreneurial skills into the business. Their basic strategy was to hire cheap, unapprenticed labour who worked for them or their subcontractors at home. Only the highly skilled cutting operations were carried out on their premises. But journeymen in bespoke tailoring also did home-work for them, especially during the slack season of the made-to-order industry. Confection, producing for anonymous sale, could work the year round.

A few simple figures from the enquiry on Parisian industry in 1847 tell the story of what happened during the July Monarchy.[e] In that year, Parisian tailoring as a whole had gross sales of over 80 million francs, and confection accounted for a third of it. The share of the bespoke tailors[f] was 60 per cent. Another 7 per cent derived from the activity of subcontractors called *appiéceurs*, many of whom also worked for the ready-made magnates. The workforce in bespoke tailoring was 9,765 people, while ready-made employed a disproportionately high number, 7,445, indicating an important fact: ready-made was labour-intensive and relied on cheap labour for its success. The number of confectionneurs in Paris was a mere 223 while that of master bespoke tailors was 3,012. The *confectionneurs'* gross sales averaged 125,000 francs and the bespoke tailors only 16,000. But the *merchant*-tailor was not the one who paid with the rise of ready-made. Among all tailoring firms exceeding 100,000 francs of business per year, fifty-six bespoke tailors were represented, and the total number of merchant tailors had increased by 250 per cent since 1830.

But the vast majority of bespoke tailors were very small operators. Three-fifths had gross sales of less than 5,000 francs. Even figuring a profit margin of 20 per cent, the yearly income of a majority of bespoke master tailors in Paris was about the same as a steadily employed journeyman in the trade.[4]

Finally, the volume of business in the whole industry had just about doubled since 1825. The lion's share of this went to the ready-made business to be sure, but the big merchant tailor in bespoke tailoring got his due as well.

Revolutions in marketing and industrial structure had occurred. The small master either fell into the ranks of the wage-earners or eked out an existence against insurmountable odds. Or he became a subcontractor of sweated labour. On the other hand, the merchant-tailors survived by accentuating trends they had begun and by copying the capitalist practices of the confectionneurs. By 1848 over half of their workforce worked at home and around 40 per cent of their workers were women. They also took on subcontracted labour as heavily as the ready-made people. The great new force, then, in the wage-earning categories of tailoring was sweated labour. Their wages were 60 per cent of that of the in-shop journeyman, they were totally unorganized and their hours totally unregulated.

What happened to the work life of the journeyman tailor? First, his skill level deteriorated. The old system called upon the shop journeyman to learn every aspect of the trade, but the new one led to specialization and an elaborate division of labour. Only an elite of cutters maintained the old diversity of knowledge. Rationalization, efficiency, lower costs – and, for the worker, monotony and, above all, *partial* training – became the hallmarks of the trade. Only the small shops retained the tradition of multi-skilled activities, but they were being crushed. Then there was the insecurity of employment. Tailoring had always been seasonal – heavy demand in the spring and autumn. But the competition of ready-made goods caused *bespoke* employers to push harder in rush times, lay off more and earlier in slack. Finally, journeyman's wages declined after 1830 under the inevitable calculus of labour competition. The misery of sweated labour produced the hardship of the journeyman shopworker.

Whom did the journeymen attack? At first, their direct employers, the bespoke masters. They did so largely through typical trade union activity. Around 1846 and especially in 1848 they increasingly turned their wrath towards confectionneurs such as Parissot and were joined by many small masters as well. Spurred on by dreams of a past independence they never really had, tailors fused together in struggle. They were artisans whose work and beings were being de-artisanized. With their corporate traditions, long urban experience, a strong sense of self-worth and – not incidentally – a high level of literacy, they joined one army in the working-class war against emergent industrial capitalism.

Tailors fought beside cabinet-makers now forced to sell cheap goods to jobbers or peddle their finer products on the streets; beside shoemakers chained to subcontractors of leather merchants, waiting in houses on call for orders or simply roaming the streets in search of customers; beside masons, carpenters and joiners no longer called to work by customers who wanted a building put up, but by building-trade entrepreneurs, or rather their subcontracted agents in the trade.

The large-city artisans of France, proletarianized by structural change, thus formed one wing of the working-class movement. But the form and ideology of their struggle reflected the peculiarities of their artisan past and the rather isolated experiences of their proletarianization. The consequence was the development of powerful and militant, yet essentially limited *craft consciousness*, seen especially in their orientation towards producers co-operatives. The ideological outcome, analysed with precision in a book by Bernard Moss, was a federalist trade socialism, or in Moss's words, 'a form of socialism that would preserve the autonomy and integrity of the trade'.[5]

Let us now turn to another world of struggle against industrial capitalism in mid-nineteenth-century France, the small, old, mono-industrial city. Here, the pressures of structural change often went deep into the eighteenth century and resulted in the meshing together of functionally separate crafts as their traditional corporative autonomy was destroyed. In contrast to the large city artisans, workers in such towns were thrown together by objective forces of industrial change and forged a unity of purpose which emphasized intercraft co-operation and the struggle for control of the entire community. They were, I suppose one might say, 'truer' proletarians than the Parisian tailors and their kin; they might be viewed as more exact prototypes of the modern industrial proletariat, harbingers as they were of industrial unionism and class-conscious socialism. But if large-city artisans operated in relative craft isolation, they did so in relative geographical isolation. Lodève provides an excellent laboratory for assessing the various processes at work. Some of my preliminary findings about this Languedoc[8] city may prove useful in stimulating further thought on this pattern of proletarianization.

The main centre of woollen cloth production for the army, which ensured a secure if highly fluctuating market, Lodève was a bustling town of 12,000 people in 1851. Fully 45 per cent of the city's active population found employment in the woollens industry, another 2 per cent owned it, and most of its artisans, shopkeepers and professionals owed their livelihood to it. Lodève had a large agricultural population that also had various ties with the industry. Lodève was and is a physically small city – one can walk across it in any direction in ten minutes. Its housing is densely packed together, opening up only along the quays of the Lergue and Solandres rivers, the lifeblood of the industry with their clear waters and rapid flow, and in the Place St Fulcran before the ancient cathedral and the episcopal palace that became the city hall during the French Revolution. In the mid-nineteenth century the town was socially segregated. The large houses of the *fabricants* (the owners) and professionals were located in the upper town near St Fulcran. The workshops and shops of the artisans and retailers dotted the central city. Woollens workers were concentrated in the lower city – the old parish of St Pierre – and especially in the faubourgs across the rivers Montbrun and Carmes. The agricultural workers and the small number of peasant proprietors tended to be located in the peripheral areas of the city, though they were found in significant numbers in all *quartiers*.[6]

Such was the general look of Lodève in the mid-nineteenth century. What went on inside its confines? Essentially, a class struggle of epic proportions. . . . Space prevents a full presentation of the evidence proving the proletarian character of this city. But a few key points can be stressed. Hardly a year passed between 1821 and 1848 in which *some* kind of collective working-class action did not occur. Fully-fledged work stoppages in the woollens industry occurred in twelve of those twenty-seven years. These strikes share several important characteristics.[7] First, all occurred when the *fabrique*[h] was besieged with orders. Woollens workers did not strike defensively. Second, strike activity, while generally initiated by workers in a particular craft (such as the croppers in 1821 or the spinners in 1831 or the weavers in 1834 and 1845) won universal support in the other woollens crafts. Moreover, women workers often stood at the forefront of the movement – as in 1821, when women pelted gendarmes and scabs with stones. And non-woollens workers were involved in crowd manifestations associated with the strikes, while retail merchants were generous with credit during strike periods. If scabs were to be found, they had to be imported. Third, if Luddism, the struggle against the machine, went on, it occurred in the context of a complex of other issues. In 1821, croppers and their allies actually managed to stop the introduction of the first *tondeuse*, or cropping machine, into Lodève, but the action also led to demands by spinners and weavers for pay increases, which came the following year with a new strike. The tondeuse arrived successfully in 1823 and provoked a strike, the outcome of which guaranteed no lay-offs, past wage levels and worker training in the operation and maintenance of the machine. The strikes of 1831–4 and 1839–40 had nothing at all to do with machinery, being focused instead on regaining earlier piece-rates, equalizing pay from workshop to workshop and bettering working conditions among weavers and spinners. The great 1845 strike *began* as a reaction to the introduction of the power loom, but soon gave way to a general struggle over piece-rates, fine systems and a host of work-related grievances. The king's prosecutor (*procureur du roi*), hardly a friend of the workers, finally declared after a long discussion with the bosses that the real goal of the fabricants in their massive efforts to break the strike was not specifically to protect or enhance their profits, but that for them 'it was a question of *mastery*, that it was necessary for a master to govern his workers, failing which the latter would not work'. And machinery was a means more surely to effectuate that end. For Lodève workers, then, the struggle against the machine was not the last gasp of dying artisans, but a sophisticated and variegated response to their employers' efforts to enhance their dominant position. Fourth, and perhaps most important, throughout this period, the Lodève woollens workers maintained associational links, the concrete dimensions and structures of which completely eluded police surveillance. As with the Adam assassination,[i] officials *knew* they were there but could not prosecute. The subprefect[j] lamented in 1834 that 'the workers employed in woollens manufacture are associated by *corps d'état* or profession'. Moreover, 'they are associated as a mass in ways impossible to determine'.[8] One has the impression of an incredible network of professional, social and familial links, all intertwined, that produced virtually instantaneous action when needed.

Strike strategy indicated an elaborate organizational base. For example, the strike of 1834, begun by handloom weavers objecting to an uncompensated increase in the size of the cloth, quickly turned to demands for increases beyond the compensation. A single, twenty-four-loom weavers' shed, that of Jourdan, was selected as the focus, and its strikers were monetarily supported by the rest of the weavers. As Jourdan, pressed with heavy orders, began to waver, his machine spinners and carders went out, and the weavers upped their demands to include an *indemnity* for the time they had lost while on strike! This was followed by another selective strike of spinners at Pascal's. The subprefect was convinced that this intercraft action was planned in advance and supported by the bulk of the town's woollens workers, who would then seek to generalize the wage standards set at Jourdan's. This became clear when, on 27 January 1834, a huge demonstration of 700 Lodève workers was organized to protest the failure of the mayor to validate work passports of four Jourdan weavers who wanted to go to Bédarieux to seek work. What occurred at the end of the march, on the route to Bédarieux, symbolizes the dimensions of the class struggle in Lodève. The national guard had not been called out because it was unreliable; as a police report noted, the guardsmen 'are mostly proprietors and artisans who are little disposed to show favor to the fabricants against the workers'. Thus only the subprefect Brun and a few gendarmes were there to meet the crowd. Brun declared the entire body of marchers under arrest, to which their leader, the weaver Jacquesjean, responded that they were merely exercising their historic rights as *compagnons* to see their

89

brothers off on the Tour de France!^{k} The humour of it all escaped Brun, as did the next incident: a spinner named Ollier dashed from the crowd, grabbed one of the *garde champêtre's*^{l} sword and scurried back, waving it over his head to the laughter of 700 voices. The chief of police, a squat retired army captain and relative of the powerful Fabreguettes fabricant family, saved some face for the other side by wading into the crowd and retrieving it. Brun then proceeded to try to arrest the front row of demonstrators, who quickly pinned his arms to his sides and then quietly disarmed the motley band of justice's defenders. The farce was over. Brun and his companions were left sputtering in the twilight as the crowd disappeared into the streets, courts and doorways of the city.

The effect of this action was twofold. First, the fabricants caved in, for the rush of orders was too great. They even promised that no arrests would be made in connection with the demonstration. But, second, Brun and his superiors in Montpellier and Paris refused to submit to such intimidation. Thus, on 5 February an attempt to arrest the four weavers now back at work *chez* Jourdan resulted in a two-day, clearly political strike in which the entire woollens industry was closed down in a stroke. It was now a struggle for the very soul of the town. In the dénouement, the woollens workers did not win, as the town was infested with troops. But neither did they lose. Their economic strike demands had been met, their collective strength in the community was made obvious and they had gained an important psychological edge.[9] A working-class presence was manifest.

And this manifestation went well beyond strikes: anticlerical demonstrations, July Revolution festivals, political meetings in the countryside, constant café gatherings, numerous examples of in-shop protests under the clear direction of shop stewards and dozens of other activities demonstrated the unified and determined struggle for power unfolding under the July Monarchy.[10] And during the Second Republic,^{m} the Lodève proletariat came to democratic socialism *en masse*, became the only working class in France simply to take over the writing of the cantonal enquiry on agricultural and industrial work, and then defied the reaction through outright murder, secret societies and finally resistance to the *coup d'état*.^{n}

The central question is how did it get that way? This is a

more complicated problem than locating the foundations of craft consciousness among proletarianizing artisans, for while changing work structures stimulated the process of proletarianization and impelled this working class towards unity, socio-demographic, ecological and general community structural considerations played just as important a part. But there was a clear chronology. The years from 1740 to around 1800 comprised the main period for changes in work structure and the power relations on the job. This transformation occurred before machine technology had made any significant impact at all and largely in the political context of the Old Regime. The second set of factors, those relating to community structure seem to date from around 1780 and continue to function in the making of this working class down to the Second Republic.

Let us briefly outline the first.[11] Seventeen twenty-nine is probably the key date in the history of Lodève, for in that year Cardinal Fleury,° her most famous native son, directed the bulk of the army orders for woollen cloth to this little city of about 4,000 souls, and the peculiar rhythm of the city's industrial life was established. The sharp ebb and flow of orders, which followed the military situation, created constant boom and bust alterations.

In the first years of the eighteenth century, before the new army demand, the structure of production in Lodève was typically corporative: the main stages of manufacturing were controlled by guilds whose regulations were recognized under public law. And by law, all processes were to take place within the city. The merchant–manufacturers, or fabricants, formed the first and most influential guild. They had already gained full control over the materials of production and, in typical fashion, put out the wool and carried it through all the stages of manufacture, finally marketing the finished cloth. The first steps of production – degreasing, washing, fluffing and sorting – were carried out by wage-earning employees of the fabricants (mainly women) who worked in the fabricants' warehouses and in the shallow beds in the rivers nearby. The prepared wool was then put out on a contractual basis to carders whose guild structure was already weak at the opening of the century, having been unable to prevent non-guildsmen from entering the trade. The fabricants had paved the way by offering to supply expensive carding tools and oil to the interlopers. Both guild and non-guild carders subcontracted almost exclusively female home labour for spinning, generally providing them with their wheels. This large labour force worked for piece-wages.

The weaver's guild commanded the next step in the process. Master weavers maintained their own shops, generally owned their looms and usually kept one journeyman and one apprentice. It was a male craft. They often contracted with specialists who had rights, through the guild, to string the warp of the loom and bathe the finished warp in light glue. Such operations, however, might also be done by family members. An efficient shop would have at least two looms. Weavers were never wealthy, but were without question the hub of the industry. The legal support of their guild regulations, control over access to mastership and the maintenance of monopoly rights over cloth bearing the *marque de Lodève*[P] – these were the keys to their independence and power. Their confrérie, with its patron saints, processions, ceremonies and social events, cemented their bond of brotherhood.

The cloth was then returned to the fabricants' warehouses and submitted to *épotoyage*, the pulling of woof threads to remove irregularities, done by women who doubled as sorters and were in the direct employ of the fabricant. Fulling came next and was carried out in water-powered mills generally owned by the fabricants. These mills were manned by skilled managers whose contractual relations with the fabricants varied widely.

The finishing processes were turned over to the true elite of producers in Lodève and members of the strongest guild beneath that of the fabricants, the *pareurs* or teaselers. They took the rough cloth from the fulling process through the final stages of teasing, cropping, squaring and folding. The cloth was then returned to the warehouse for the final pressing. All the skilled men associated with the finishing process contracted with master pareurs and were associated in their guild. They tended to be richer than weavers and like them, were protected through their guild regulations and their confrérie. Dyers, less prominent in Lodève because of the nature of its product, shared the characteristics of the fullers.

Prices of all work involving guild interrelationships were set by elaborate codes agreed upon by the guilds through the arbitration of the royal inspector. Workers outside guild protection were paid according to the laws of supply and demand, as was subcontracted labour. Agreement between fabricants and fullers and dyers responded to market conditions as well. Final quality control was exclusively in the hands of the *jurés-gardes*, a six-man elected board of fabricants who reported to the inspector.

Lodève's woollens industry thus operated on the basis of a hodgepodge of market and corporative principles in which the proletarian characteristics of its workforce were minimal.

The transformation of the eighteenth century was decisive. It evolved in two basic stages: first, the drastic alterations accompanying the initial impact of large army orders and most keenly felt during the War of Austrian Succession,[q] which obliterated the authority of the weavers' and pareurs' guilds; and, second, the more subtle changes occurring during and after the American War for Independence that commenced the trent towards a factory system without machines.

The first was marked by the collapse of the legal buttresses supporting the position of the two key producers' guilds. The 1730s witnessed the proliferation of rural carding and spinning, which was then followed by rural weaving. The latter developed especially in the early 1740s when orders doubled virtually overnight. It was illegal, but the law turned a deaf ear to the Lodève weavers. Next came the push by fabricants to get individual master weavers to work for only one manufacturer, which they contrived by offering generous advances and catching many weavers in a form of peonage. Significant pay differentials began to emerge. Then came the inevitable – the hiring of non-guild weavers in Lodève itself, largely migrants from weaving villages. One can imagine their reception in the weavers' community at the time, but the law – ultimately validated by the Estates of Languedoc[r] – supported the fabricants' drive for free enterprise. At the same time, entrance into the fabricants' guild became increasingly difficult, above all due to the sky-rocketing cost of the mastership fee: 300 livres in 1708, it rose to 1,050 livres by 1749, but with the crucial proviso that the sons of fabricants would be required to pay a mere 200.[12] The fabricants were becoming a closed caste. The merchant–manufacturers' struggle against the pareurs followed a pattern similar to that against the weavers, but since rural competition was largely impossible given the skill requirements of the finishing crafts, the path was more difficult. Nevertheless, during the 1740s, the same policies of entrapment and hiring non-guild workers ensued. To a vociferous protest by the pareurs, the inspector general in Montpellier issued this chilling decision: 'Contract, day, and pieceworkers of this province would like to lord it over those who give them subsistence. It would not be convenient to send their request further, a request that must only be answered by a resounding no!'[13] Lyonnais silk-weavers had a similar experience at about the same time. Maurice Garden's comments regarding the changing face of the law under the impact of economic expansion in the eighteenth century are well taken.[14]

The guilds were broken and the logic of industrial capitalism took hold in Lodève. Stage two added at least four new ingredients. First and above all, was the drive to concentrate carders, weavers, pareurs and their adjunct crafts into factory-like contexts under the eye of the boss and operating on his time schedule. The process was nearing completion by the time of the revolution, as indicated by a petition to the Convention[s] from distraught home workers.[15] Second was the employment of female workers in weaving. The word *tisserande*[t] would have been a contradiction in terms in 1740. By 1800 approximately one-fourth of the weavers of Lodève were women, although they may not have put in the same hours annually as the men. Third, the segregation of housing accentuated during the second half of the century, especially since the population of Lodève had increased by about 3,000. In 1798, 34 per cent of Lodève's population were migrants, the vast majority of whom came to the city as young adults. They located where rentals were cheap – in the teeming parish of St Pierre and especially in the faubourgs. The patterns of human ecology of 1851 were well in place by 1800. Fourth, the origins of migrants who are found in the woollens trade in 1798 changed significantly from the time of the American Revolution on, while the rural putting-out system in the Lodève area declined. A *reurbanization* of the industry was occurring. Manufacturers, having broken the guilds, now reduced their reliance on the more distant and less stable rural workforce and increasingly sought experienced urban weavers willing to accept proletarian status. These they found: 70 per cent of the migrant weavers who arrived in Lodève after 1778 came from *depressed* woollens centres still operating under modified corporative structures – towns such as St Pons, Riols, St Chinian, Lacaune and St Affrique, or from towns which were themselves following the Lodève pattern, such as Clermont and Bédarieux. Migrants from distraught outworking villages arrived as well, but their success rates as measured by home ownership were not nearly that of the previous generation. Lodève belonged to the fabricants; they had a proletarianized population to do their bidding.[16]

But by the 1820s, and particularly by the 1830s, this population increasingly refused to do their bidding. Bear in mind that during the Napoleonic years,[17] Lodève prospered. Army orders were naturally high, but manpower relatively scarce. This improved the bargaining position of the woollens workers, especially in terms of wages, but it also stimulated further efforts on the part of the fabricants to rationalize production. During this era, carding and spinning underwent significant mechanization and the use of female labour in hand loom weaving sheds accelerated. Neither trend appears to have provoked much protest for two interconnected reasons: the manner in which labour was redeployed and the maintenance of levels of family earnings. Hand carders, already more proletarianized than any other craft, became carding and spinning machine tenders, indeed foremen, often for the same fabricant for whom they worked as hand carders. The female hand spinners also found work in mechanical spinneries, as did their children. In many cases it must have been simply a matter of whole families moving from non-mechanized to mechanized work. The spinning factories were small, and the machines carried a low number of spindles and were crude devices in need of constant attention from workers. Redundant female hand spinners, moreover, could easily move into hand loom weaving jobs. The central fact, I think, was that the operation of the workers' family economy could remain intact. Overall – the second point – what we are witnessing is the historic trade-off of pay, on the one hand, for job reclassification involving greater domination by the boss, on the other. In general, then, the empire saw some fairly severe alterations of work structure, but also, because of the constancy of employment and decent pay, took on the allure of a kind of 'golden age'. It was followed by severely depressed conditions, from 1814 to

95

1821, which carries us up to the beginning of Lodève's age of proletarian revolt.[17]

But the proletarian character of this city was for all intents and purposes fixed before these two decades of mechanization, prosperity and collapse. Let me lay out some of the evidence demonstrating the level of working-class integration – bases for the subjective unity of this proletariat – that I have been able to draw from the remarkable census of 1798. This census, taken for unknown local reasons, is to my knowledge without parallel in France at this early date and includes (besides normal information such as age, sex, occupation, family relationships, household and house data) home ownership, precise birthplace *and* the number of years migrants had been in Lodève at that date. It is a gold mine, and I am still in the process of analysing the mass of information that it can yield.[18]

The central question here is this: to what extent was the in-migrant population of Lodève integrated into its working class? All the evidence in the world proving that changing structures of work and industrial organization were pushing towards the formation of a proletariat does not necessarily demonstrate that proletarian unity occurred. People might face precisely the same objective conditions on the job, be thoroughly similar in their income status and hate each other's guts. Just talk to Black and Polish workers in Detroit's Dodge Main. Migrants, the circumstances of their arrival, their role in the economy, their cultural peculiarities, their manner of living and relating to the host population and many other factors, can and have historically muddied the clearest of objective analyses of why a conscious proletariat *ought* to exist in any given context. . . .

The age, character and marriage patterns of migrants, however, provide the surest evidence of my thesis. Migrants to Lodève, male or female, wherever they came from, whenever they came, overwhelmingly arrived as single young adults. They migrated for work-related reasons and they married in Lodève generally after several years of residence. Whom did they marry? Men and women from back home? Almost never. At least other migrants? No – not normally – and here is the central point. Migrants, male and female, tended to tie themselves to established Lodève families through the process of marriage, except again among agricultural workers. Special attention should be drawn to male woollens workers. Out of ninety-eight migrants in the trade who were married (another seventy were not), seventy-five had married Lodève women, and only two of those who married migrants had wed a woman from 'back home'. Moreover, marriage records indicate a strong tendency among migrant woollens workers to marry daughters of Lodève woollens workers.[19] Finally, female migrants were perfectly acceptable wives for Lodève-born woollens workers. One-third of their marriages were contracted with migrants. . . .

CONCLUSION

This comparative analysis of two early patterns of proletarianization suggests several conclusions. In both cases, we are dealing with the collapse of corporative modes of production as capitalist practices pervade the manufacturing process. The structural change in the organization of production precedes any major technological change and indeed paves the way for it. And the legal framework in which such changes occur is crucial – for Parisian tailoring, it was the licence given to *laissez-faire* resulting from the French Revolution, but for Lodève, an earlier, more subtle process involving a series of specific decisions in the mid-eighteenth century. In general, then, the structural transformations in both cases bear marked similarities, although they operate on a different timetable. But this difference is fundamental, as is the totally different social and geographical context in which the transformation occurs. Both the tailors' and the Lodève movements reached a climax at roughly the same time – the mid-nineteenth century. Yet the tailors were at that point in the full throes of de-artisanization in a context in which their corporate traditions continued to play a basic role in their mentality. They did not try to organize their entire industry against capitalist exploitation. In fact they regarded the sweated labour produced by merchant-tailors and ready-made entrepreneurs as their enemies. More telling still is the fact that as the Clichy producers' co-operative achieved success in 1849, it too began to *hire* sweated labour. Suggestions of antagonism against new workers outside the corporation were certainly there in eighteenth-century Lodève, but by the mid-nineteenth century virtually all vestiges of corporate exclusivism had disappeared. Thus, on the one hand, the tailors and other large-city artisans undergoing proletarian-ization bequeath to the later nineteenth-century labour move-ment a powerful ideology of craft-conscious trade socialism, whereas, on the other, Lodève workers and their brethren in small, old industrial towns leave an inheritance of vociferous class consciousness, industrial unionism and democratic social-ism broadly conceived. But all this existed in miniature. The established, intensively interactive and industrially integrated city that produced this true proletariat was, after all, very small and relatively isolated. The final irony was that Lodève did not survive as an industrial city in the later nineteenth century. One can argue that the specialized nature of its market, the developing obsolescence of its technology, the competition of the north, the advance of the vine in the south and even the betrayal of its governmental patron, Michel Chevalier, were responsible for this collapse. But figuring into every aspect of such arguments was an overriding fact: this was a proletarian city and its proletariat was *too* powerful.

I would like to conclude with a methodological comment. In recent years, considerable attention has been devoted to the study of work structure in analysing the process of proletarian-ization. Such analysis has been used to explain (or at least clarify) aspects of worker behaviour that otherwise seem prob-lematic. It has been an important trend in historical study, and I have been party to it. But we must avoid becoming entrapped by such an approach, for it is very inviting to think that if one has understood the working world of workers, their changing relations with their bosses and the forms of organization that arise out of work situations, one has understood the working class. But clearly that is not enough, any more than an earlier generation's focus on 'the standard-of-living question', trade union development or labour politics was enough. Nothing short of an attempt to grasp the *whole* of the working class experience in its manifold variety is called for. . . .

EDITOR'S NOTES

a A form of intensive factory management advocated by the Ameri-can engineer, Frederick Taylor, at the end of the nineteenth century.

b Johnson uses the terms 'industrial' and 'mono-industrial' in the nineteenth-century sense. He would not want the reader to assume that industry involved machine production. Manufacturing by hand was the rule.

c Literally, 'mushroom cities'. These cities grew rapidly from villages as a result of industrial development.

d That is, a guild organization, with fixed rules for production, employment and so on.

e The government in France between 1830 and 1848, under King Louis-Philippe.

f The tailors who made complete suits in the traditional manner; in contrast to the partially-trained workers who worked in the ready-to-wear sector.

g The province in which Lodève was located.

h The guild-like organization representing the woollen industry.

i Johnson mentioned this murder in a paragraph which has been omitted. Adam was a police officer who had been stabbed by workers during a labour dispute in 1849.

j A local officer of the central government.

k The traditional travel which young journeymen undertook to seek employment and develop their skills.

l A village police officer.

m The democratic regime in France created by the February Revolution of 1848 and ended when President Louis-Napoleon Bonaparte made himself emperor in 1852.

n Louis-Napoleon, elected president in December 1848, pursued increasingly regressive policies and finally ended constitutional democracy with his *coup d'état* in December 1851.

o Chief minister to King Louis XV between 1726 and 1743.

p The trademark guaranteeing that the cloth had been produced under proper regulations.

q 1740–8.

r The regional assembly which shared administration of the province with the Crown.

s The democratic assembly during radical phase of the revolution, 1792 to 1795.

t Female weaver.

u 1799–1815.

NOTES

From Christopher H. Johnson, 'Patterns of proletarianization: Parisian tailors and Lodève woolen workers', in John M. Merriman (ed.), *Consciousness and Class Experience in Nineteenth-Century Europe* (New York, 1979): 65–84. Copyright © 1979 by Holmes & Meier Publishers, Inc. Reprinted by permission of the publisher. Ellipses are used at the request of the publisher.

1 This paragraph summarizes a decade of research and theorizing.

The essence of the argument, however, is perhaps best presented by Stephen A. Marglin, 'What do bosses do?: the origins and functions of hierarchy in capitalist production', *Union of Radical Political Economists*, 6 (summer 1974): 60–112. On proto-industrialization, the recent studies of Franklin Mendels are important, but the best summary of the problem and the most extensive bibliography may be found in Jürgen Schlumbohm's 'Productivity of labour, process of production, and relations of production: some remarks on stagnation and progress in European rural industries (17th–19th centuries)', a working paper available from the Max Planck-Institut für Geschichte, Göttingen, Germany.

2 See Christopher H. Johnson, *Utopian Communism in France* (Ithaca, NY, 1974): esp. ch. 5.

3 See C. H. Johnson, 'Economic change and artisan discontent: the tailors' history, 1800–48', in Roger Price (ed.), *Revolution and Reaction* (London, 1975): 87–114, for a detailed examination of the process outlined here. The reader is referred to that article for complete source citations.

4 The main statistical sources are: Chambre de Commerce de Paris, *Statistique de l'industrie à Paris résultant de l'enquête faite par la Chambre de Commerce pour les années 1847–1848* (Paris, 1851): 285–305; and Lémann, confectionneur, *De l'industrie des vêtements confectionnés en France* (Paris, 1857): *passim*.

5 Bernard H. Moss, *The Origins of the French Labor Movement: The Socialism of Skilled Workers* (Berkeley, Calif., 1976).

6 These general remarks are drawn from a wide range of sources and personal experience, but the census of 1851 (Archives départementales, Hérault, 115M28/1) is the main base of the figures.

7 All relevant archival citations relating to this section would occupy several pages. Thus only the most voluminous and comprehensive cartons are noted here. Archives nationales, BB[18]1221, 1376, 1389 and 1429; Archives départementales, Hérault, 39M119 and 125 (some 800 pieces, 'Grèves de Lodève') and 20X16; Archives communales de Lodève 7F1 ('Grèves, coalitions').

8 Archives départementales, Hérault, 39M125.

9 This fascinating story is drawn from copies of police reports, the mayor's report and various detailed reports from Brun, the *procureur de roi* in Lodève, to his superior in Montpellier, and provides a sample of the incredible detail that my documentation can yield. The relevant sources are Archives départementales, Hérault 39M125 and Archives communales, Lodève 7F1.

10 Archives communales, Lodève 7F1, 111, 116, 1112, Q22; Archives départementales, Hérault 39M8, 33, 53, 107, 109, 114, 115, 121, 125, 127, 128, 132, 134, 140, 141.

11 Unless otherwise noted, the following analysis of mid-eighteenth-century Lodève is based on information drawn from Emile Appolis, *Un pays langueducien au milieu du XVIIIe siècle: le diocèse civil de Lodève* (Albi, 1951); Ernest Martin, *Histoire de la ville de Lodève*, 2 vols (Montpellier, 1900), vol. II; E. Martin (ed.), *Le Cartu-*

laire de Lodève (Montpellier, 1900); and Léon Dutil, *L'Etat économique du Languedoc à la fin de l'ancien régime* (Paris, 1911): 277–444.

12 Archives départementales, Hérault C2792.

13 Archives départementales, Hérault C2424.

14 Maurice Garden, *Lyon et les lyonnais au XVIIIe siècle* (Paris, n.d.): esp. 582–92.

15 'Les Tisserands de Lodève aux citoyens composants la Commission des subsistances à Paris', (n.d., but sometime in the Year II), Archives nationales, $F^{12}1389$–90.

16 The key source for the foregoing section is a census taken in the Year VI (described in the text below) that I discovered in the Archives communales de Lodève (1F2). Also important, however, are *plaintes et placets*, Archives départementales, Hérault C6766 and C6767.

17 Archives départementales, Hérault, 132M1–6; 131M19. Archives communales, Lodève, 1G2–7, 64–73 (Patentes).

18 What follows is based, to a significant extent, on this census (see note 36). At the time of this writing, the calculations were done by hand. This census is currently being put in machine-readable form. My thanks to Louise Tilly for help in coding procedures.

19 Etat civil de Lodève, Registres de mariage, 1802–6. (No classification: Mairie de Lodève.)

6

DRINK AND INDUSTRIAL DISCIPLINE IN NINETEENTH-CENTURY GERMANY

James S. Roberts

The work regime in factories during the early industrial era has frequently been evoked, though rarely studied in detail. Textbooks have often cited the draconian rules, the heavy fines, the frenzied work pace, the dangerously-exposed machine parts, and the sexual favours unscrupulous foremen demanded from powerless workers. Recall that David Landes viewed the new sort of workforce – a highly regimented and undifferentiated mass of labourers – as an innovation of the Industrial Revolution. Presumably, the rise of factory production forced labourers to abandon their loose pre-industrial habits and work tirelessly as adjuncts of machines.

As Cannadine's essay makes clear, interpretations of the Industrial Revolution are closely tied to assumptions about economic growth. This concern brought scholars to strike an ambiguous tone regarding the iron factory discipline. On the one hand, there was abundant reason to lament (in retrospect) the abuses and sympathize with hard-pressed wage-earners. On the other hand – and less explicitly – authors frequently identified with managers as agents of rationality and efficiency. Management was, after all, raising productivity and creating wealth. An implicit assumption in the literature was that breaking workers of their shiftless, pre-industrial ways was a regrettable, brutal, but necessary task.

Recent research on factory management has come to new conclusions. It seems that most nineteenth-century factories were loosely integrated. Craft methods of production were incorporated into manufacturing. Industrial artisans, by virtue of their skills and know-how, had power over their employers. Indeed, some scholars argue that 'craft control' or 'worker control' was at least as important as managerial control (which we, today, take to be natural and inevitable) until the late nineteenth century, and often beyond that.

James Roberts brings a clever and suggestive focus to the study of factory labour. He uses the issue of alcoholic consumption to illuminate factory discipline. Roberts's study raises intriguing questions about the prevalence of so-called pre-industrial habits in modern industry. The essay also forces a questioning of management's role as the agent of modernization. Readers must sort through the differences that emerge between Roberts's essay and the textbook's picture of 'dark, satanic mills'.

* * *

Sidney Pollard, E. P. Thompson and others have shown that the men and women who entered the industrial labour force in the eighteenth and nineteenth centuries, whether recruited from the urban craft traditions, cottage industry or the surplus population of the countryside, brought with them habits and values hostile to the demands of modern industry.[1] The discipline essential to the new system of production thus required the destruction of familiar work rhythms, themselves entwined with customary material expectations and patterns of sociability. Modern industry brought instead the 'time thrift' imposed by the factory clock, an unremitting pace of work set by interlocking mechanical processes and the radical divorce of the experience of work from wider realms of human activity.

There can be little doubt that these were the long-term tendencies in those countries and in those industries most affected by the factory system and machine production. But at the same time we must remember, as this discussion of the Drink Question at the workplace is meant to show, that what was logically implicit in the new system of production was seldom – if ever – fully realized. The transformation of work was gradual and uneven, never fitting fully the ideal types historians have constructed to point up the contrast between industrial and pre-industrial labour.

An examination of the Drink Question at the workplace can illuminate in several ways the nature of industrial work discipline and the process by which it was created and maintained. The Drink Question encompassed all the major problems of industrial work discipline, from inefficiency and insubordination on the job to the backward bending supply curve of labour that bedevilled industrial employers in one form or another throughout the nineteenth century. Its study sheds light both on the experience of work as Germany industrialized and on the conflicts between workers and employers to control the industrial labour process. For workers, alcoholic beverages had many uses and meanings. Alcohol was a thirst quencher and dietary supplement, a narcotic and a stimulant. But just as important as these 'instrumental' functions of drinking on the job were alcohol's social roles, for as in most other cultures, communal drinking practices formed a tangible social bond among working men. For employers, on the other hand, the use of alcohol at the workplace presented itself ultimately as a problem, as an obstacle to industrial work discipline. Thus the battle lines were drawn. Employers tried to eliminate alcohol from the workplace, while many workers insisted on their right to drink.

The discussion that follows is based on a wide variety of sources – factory inspectorate reports, temperance literature, the socialist and trade union press and medical and social-scientific writings on the Drink Question. Each of these sources is by itself fragmentary and incomplete, but taken together they provide a very considerable record of working-class drinking behaviour and the efforts of employers and others to curtail it. Nevertheless, as is nearly always the case, this record is by no means as complete as the historian would like, and the account that follows can pretend to do no more than provide a basic outline of trends and themes involved in this chapter of the history of labour relations. Detailed local studies would no doubt uncover variations in the facts and tentative conclusions presented here, but even this preliminary discussion of drink and industrial work discipline sheds some interesting light on nineteenth-century labour history.

Conceived in ideal–typical terms, alcohol and industry did not mix. Conducive to absenteeism, accidents, inefficiency and insubordination, working-class drinking was a natural obstacle to the rationally calculating employer seeking to discipline his workforce. In fact, however, employers only gradually took up the fight against alcohol, and drinking patterns and work rhythms remained closely intertwined in some industries well into the twentieth century. Pre-industrial habits and attitudes lived on into the industrial era. This was true both of employers' attitudes to the drinking of their workers, which they often condoned and even abetted, and of workers' belief about alcohol and their custom of using it on the job.

The association between work and drink predated modern industry. The urban and rural craft traditions allowed for frequent drinking. In the pre-industrial economy, the pace of work could be varied according to life's other demands and the working day punctuated with discussion, song and drink.[2] On the job, alcohol served both as a stimulant and thirst quencher and as a medium of social exchange in the informal breaks and elaborate rituals that marked the progress of apprentices and journeymen through the course of their training and from shop to shop. At this point, drinking patterns were more likely to involve master craftsmen and the journeymen and apprentices in their shops in a common social ritual than to divide employer from employee. In the countryside, too, alcohol was closely tied to the rhythm of work, especially after the proliferation of rural distilleries in the decades after 1815.[3] Agricultural labourers consumed small quantities of alcohol throughout the working day.

In the new industrial setting, alcohol continued to meet – if only imperfectly – a variety of needs, both physiological and social, of the emerging working class. Workers drank on the job for a complicated variety of reasons. Many saw in alcohol a valuable nutrient and thirst quencher.[4] Alcohol's physiological uses were strongly associated with particular occupations, where the conditions of work were harsh and the work itself physically strenuous. A. H. Stehr, a physician and economist, investigated the relationship between alcohol consumption and industrial productivity in the early twentieth century and remarked that 'it is invariably the same categories of workers . . . who claim that they cannot perform their usual work without alcohol'.[5] Stehr cited as examples workers exposed to high temperatures like glass-blowers, foundry workers and brick-makers; carters, quarrymen and construction workers who worked outdoors; and tile-makers, potters, masons and chemical workers, who were exposed to irritating dust or noxious fumes. Such connections were noted throughout the nineteenth century.

But in addition to the actual conditions of work, powerful social traditions also led workers to consume alcohol on the job. Particularly in the early phases of industrialization, when work took up the lion's share of each waking day, the occupational setting was the site of important interactions. As Rudolf Braun has noted in his insightful study of early Swiss factory workers:

> the less free time the factory worker had for the satisfaction of his social needs, the more he was forced to seek an alternative during working hours. Under the force of these circumstances, the factory workshop itself became an important arena of social life.[6]

Drinking was an important manifestation of social life on the job. Evidence of such behaviour is naturally fragmentary, but it suggests the persistence of artisanal drinking customs and more casual forms of convivial drinking at the workplace well into the twentieth century. This was particularly the case in occupations like the building trades, whose histories in the nineteenth century were less affected by mechanical than by organizational innovations. But even in more fully mechanized industries, a significant portion of the workforce continued to be recruited from the craft tradition, and it was the drinking behaviour of such workers as much as that of ordinary factory hands or unskilled workmen that frustrated many employers.[7] Reminiscing about conditions in the construction trades in the 1870s, one master mason told Wilhelm Bode, an important figure in the German temperance movement, that in those days

> Schnaps[a] had to be fetched on every occasion; when a new journeyman started work, for example, he was obliged first to provide a liter of Schnaps as his initiation [Einstand]. When an apprentice completed his first corner or curve, he too had to produce a liter of Schnaps for the others. And so it went.[8]

As late as 1913, Emanuel Wurm, a socialist parliamentary deputy especially interested in the Drink Question, noted that this kind of initiation was still all too common among German workers.[9]

Important transitions in the life cycles of individual workers and their families were also marked by drinking on the job. This was the case, for example, in Cassel, where the factory inspector reported in 1904 that 'both new arrivals and those workers who celebrate a birthday must treat their workmates to a liter of *Schnaps*, which is consumed in common and in excess of individual needs'.[10] Apart from marking important stages in the occupational and personal life cycle, social drinking probably also occurred more informally on the job. Factory owners in the Potsdam and Frankfurt a/O areas, for example, complained in 1890 about the 'Kneipereien' of their workers, who brought kegs of beer to the workplace to be consumed communally.[11]

As at other times, convivial drinking on the job was regulated by shared values and expectations. To refuse to drink was to invite ostracism and to put one's virility in question.[12] Conversely, alcohol consumption was a form of public display by which status and prowess were measured and demonstrated. Such prejudices were eroded only gradually. According to one observer, men who preferred non-alcoholic beverages actually carried them in brandy flasks in order to avoid the derision of their fellow workers.[13]

To working conditions, social traditions and beliefs about alcohol must be added the self-interest of employers in the drinking of their workers. Employers frequently provided their workers with daily rations of alcohol.[14] This practice was part of the tradition of payment in kind and was often necessary to attract a workforce at all, especially in the early years of industrial development. It is impossible to know how widespread this practice was, but it was considered eminently noteworthy when factory owners in Ruhrort and Duisburg, under the influence of the early temperance movement, broke with this tradition in the early 1840s.[15]

The myriad varieties of the truck system,[b] moreover, often made on-the-job drinking an essential part of good relations with employers and overseers. Even after employers in Prussia were specifically denied the right to sell alcohol to their workers in 1846 and the truck system was formally abolished in 1849, workers continued to face none too subtle pressures to consume alcohol to the financial benefit of their superiors.[16] Promotions, assignments and other preferments often hung in the balance. Abuses were frequent in factory canteens, especially when run for the profit of employers, overseers or members of their families. Such facilities often met the legitimate needs of the workforce for food and drink, but many of them made alcohol consumption all too easy by their liberal credit policies. This apparent generosity eventually took its toll on the workers' pocket books, for the debts so easily accumulated were reckoned up on pay-day and deducted automatically from their wage packets.

Employers used alcohol to exploit their workers in other ways as well. Early industrialists were heir to many of the same popular beliefs about alcohol as their workers. Like them, they saw in alcohol a valuable stimulant that could help hungry and exhausted men perform their work even under the most trying circumstances. Acting on these views, employers plied their workers with alcoholic beverages in the hopes of increasing their output.[17] Writing in the 1840s, a physician in Konitz, West Prussia, described the use made of spirits by the employers in his region. 'The intention', he wrote,

> Is to stimulate the poor worker to extraordinary exertion with a couple of glasses of *Branntwein*,[c] costing only a few pennies, so that the project can be completed more quickly and perhaps four times as much can be saved in wages than was spent on liquor.[18]

Such practices were perhaps appropriate to a system of production based extensively on the physical exertion of human beings, but as the organization of production changed and significant aspects of the production process were mechanized, the attitude of employers to the alcohol consumption of their workers began to change.

Changing perceptions of self-interest ultimately led most employers to the conclusion that they could extract the greatest advantage from their labourers by eliminating alcohol from the workplace rather than by providing it. It is impossible to specify exactly when employers began to alter their practice, but it appears that a reorientation was under way by the 1860s. The economic problems faced by German industry after 1873 made the need for efficient labour even more pressing.[19] By the mid-1880s, on-the-job drinking was attracting widespread public attention and had become one of the principal concerns of the revitalized German temperance movement. More and more employers, urged on by temperance reformers and many factory inspectors, began to combat on-the-job drinking in the interests of efficiency, safety and discipline.

In 1885 Viktor Böhmert, a noted National Liberal economist and prominent philanthropist, conducted a survey of industrial employers on behalf of the German Association for the Prevention of Alcohol Abuse (*Deutscher Verein gegen den Missbrauch geistiger Getränke*). Böhmert reported the same year to the group's annual conference in Dresden that German industrialists were fully aware of the need to combat the use of alcohol, especially spirits, on the job. They recognized, he said, 'that Germany will maintain its newly achieved economic position only with the help of a sober working population'.[20] Although it is difficult for the historian to specify the costs to German industry of on-the-job drinking, to most industrialists the dangers were clear. Summarizing the experiences of his informants, Böhmert reported that 'drinkers are useless for industrial purposes; they quickly become sluggish, are slow on the job, unreliable, contentious, prone to frequent illness and, in the long run, impossible to protect against the dangers of machine production'. 'They must', he concluded, 'be dismissed from the job and replaced by sober hands.'[21]

Employers resorted to a judicious combination of the carrot and the stick in their efforts to control on-the-job drinking.[22] On the positive side, industrial employers in ever increasing numbers took the initiative in making sure that non-alcoholic beverages were available to their workers. The lack of alternative beverages had long constrained workers to use alcohol as a thirst quencher and as a source of warmth and strength on the job. The provision of non-alcoholic beverages was the single most effective approach to the problem of drinking on the job, for it took account of the physiological bases of occupational drinking. Although the range of alternatives remained narrow until after the First World War, with commercially produced soft drinks too expensive for most working-class budgets, less sophisticated beverages could be equally effective.[23] In practice, this meant that workers were offered coffee, tea, milk and mineral water. In addition, greater attention was given to ordinary drinking water. Available at cost or below due to the self-interested generosity of employers, such beverages provided a satisfying and economical alternative to the more expensive beer and *Schnaps*.

Factory inspectors reported the success of such measures in factory after factory beginning in the late 1880s. Presented with a viable alternative, most workers were willing to abandon or at least curtail their alcohol consumption on the job. The royal *Eisenbahn-Wagenwerkstatt*[d] in Dortmund, for example, reported in 1904 that it had begun to offer flavoured and unflavoured mineral water to its employees at a price per bottle of 4 Pf. and 2 Pf. respectively. During the course of the first summer the beverages were available, the plant's 800 workers consumed 80,800 bottles. In addition, 102,500 litres of coffee were sold during the course of the year at a price of just 1 Pf. per litre. The result, according to the local factory inspector, was impressive: 'The use of *Schnaps* within the plant has ceased, and drunkenness on the job, which was earlier the source of frequent complaints, has not been observed since these beverages were introduced.'[24]

To the positive inducements of alternative beverages at reasonable prices was coupled the threat of harsh disciplinary measures for those who failed to comply with company regulations. Drunkenness was generally prohibited on the job, and violators were threatened with fines and sometimes immediate dismissal. Such provisions appear to have been almost universal in the factory regulations of Imperial Germany.[25] But many employers went beyond the prohibition of drunkenness and proscribed even the moderate use of alcoholic beverages on the job. Spirits were more likely to be banned than beer, but even this beverage had become the object of controls by the turn of the century.

Such measures no doubt curbed drinking to some extent, but it appears that many workers did not take kindly to these efforts to control their personal behaviour on the job. As one factory inspector from the Hanover area recalled, 'workers in those days adopted the standpoint: We do our work and what we do otherwise is no business of the factory owners'.[26] Resistance could be evidenced both in the widespread smuggling of alcoholic beverages into the workplace and even in work stoppages and strikes.[27] Of the ninety-seven firms responding to Böhmert's 1885 survey, sixty-six – employing more than 65,000 workers – had banned the use of spirits on their premises. Almost half of these firms reported serious problems with smuggling.[28] A. H. Stehr discovered similar problems when he investigated thirty firms in Breslau, Berlin and the Rhineland in 1903.[29]

The problem of smuggling indicates the limits of employers' authority and the ability of workers to evade or modify the strictures of their masters. Their power fluctuated with the state of the local labour market.[30] When labour was in short supply, restrictions could neither be introduced nor enforced. In such cases, employers had little choice but to put up with traditional drinking behaviour. Referring to the rapid industrial expansion of the *Gründerjahre*,[e] one factory inspector remembered some years later that employers were often forced to accept their workers' conceptions of labour relations on the factory floor. 'For they lacked the means', he wrote, 'to combat deep-seated abuses effectively, and it was possible to drink without limit.'[31] Similarly, the director of a large firm in Lower Alsace complained in 1901 that he was helpless to do anything about the heavy beer drinking of his employees. He was forced to conclude that 'in a certain sense the workers are more than the masters in the factory than its owner and director'.[32]

Strict control of drinking behaviour, moreover, could be a serious hindrance to the recruitment of labour. Some employers, especially in the east, declined to prohibit the use of *Schnaps* because they feared both resistance and difficulties attracting a workforce. Stehr noted of one industrial operation in Breslau, for example, that 'without permitting *Branntwein* consumption the plant can attract no workers'.[33] These were serious problems in periods of industrial expansion when the competition for labour was great and labour turnover was most costly and extensive. Indeed, when discipline and efficiency were most critical, employers were least able to enforce it. Periods of contraction in the labour market, on the other hand, were used by employers to purge the workforce of undesirable elements and to tighten labour discipline. The government inspector for the *Oberbergamtsbezirk*[f] Dortmund, for example, reported in 1901 that 'the ample supply of labor gave the mines an opportunity to cleanse the workforce of inferior elements'.[34]

If employers often met frustration when seeking to control the use of alcohol on the job, their authority was even more limited off the factory premises. Nevertheless, many industrialists were convinced, quite apart from any lingering paternalism, that what workers did in their free time was

111

crucial to their own interests. Drinking before work and on weekends was their most obvious concern. Complaints about the laxity of licensing authorities who permitted drink-sellers to cluster around the proverbial factory gates were legion, largely because workers often refreshed themselves there after their early morning trek to the workplace and during breaks in the working day.[35] Employers and temperance reformers in several major industrial regions succeeded in convincing local police authorities to prohibit liquor sales before 8 a.m., well after working men had taken up their tools. Local philanthropic societies, including temperance organizations, also addressed this problem by establishing coffee halls at the major crossroads of working-class traffic.[36] They hoped to offer workers who travelled long distances to their jobs in cold and inclement weather an attractive and inexpensive alternative to their early morning *Schnaps*.

Employers, finally, were concerned about the weekend drinking of their labour force and the disruptions caused by traditional holidays and festivals. Saint Monday[8] (*Blaue Montag*) lingered on in some branches. Absenteeism after Sundays, holidays and pay-days was abnormally high and could create serious obstacles to the efficient operation of an industrial enterprise. The factory inspector for the Düsseldorf district, for example, reported in 1876 that 'despite the bad times Saint Monday is still the most widespread evil among the workers, and the most frequently heard complaints of the employers concern it'.[37] Such complaints, if with somewhat less vehemence, could still be heard after the turn of the century. Thus the factory inspector for Bremen reported in 1902 that

> in view of the nothing less than rosy condition of the labour market, it must come as surprise that part of the workforce still clings with such tenacity to the traditional practice of skipping work, especially after Sundays and paydays.[38]

In Oberhausen, where 19,076 miners were employed during 1901, absences averaged 4 per cent per shift but reached 16 per cent after Sundays, holidays and pay-days.[39]

Employers countered these disruptive tendencies with threats, fines and firings. But here too, there were limits to their power to alter traditional patterns of behaviour. As in the case of on-the-job drinking, the authority of the industrial employer varied with the business cycle and the local supply of labour. Thus it was possible for mining companies in Gelsenkirchen to launch an offensive against Saint Monday in 1901 since the depressed state of trade made it difficult for workers to find alternative employment.[40] The threat of firing became an effective weapon under such circumstances. In the same year, however, at the nearby South-Essen coalfields, owners found themselves stymied in their efforts to combat absenteeism among their younger skilled workers. 'Since despite the unfavourable business conditions, there is no surplus of these younger workers, usally hired for specific tasks', the local factory inspector explained, 'the administration of the mines has been forced to look the other way and confine itself to monetary penalties, which demonstrably make only a very slight impression on these younger elements.'[41]

Confronted by the ineffectiveness of the means at their disposal, some employers turned to other methods of controlling drinking behaviour and the absenteeism that was seen as its result. In some areas, though not always as a result of the pressure of employers, local authorities intervened to prohibit the sale of alcoholic beverages on pay-days. This was the case in the Oppeln and Elbing districts of eastern Germany.[42] More subtle in its conception was the attempt to manipulate drinking behaviour by manipulating the pay-day. For the working-class male, pay-day, traditionally Saturday, was a day of celebration. With cash in hand and no work the next day, working men enjoyed drinking sprees that often carried over into the new working week.

In order to break the destructive association between pay-day, weekend drunkenness and absenteeism, many otherwise helpless employers played the only remaining trump in their hand: they changed the pay-day. Moving the payment of wages back to Thursday or Friday, it was hoped, would induce workers to carry their wages home instead of into the tavern. After a hard day's work the next day, the euphoria of the pay-day would have passed, the temptations to drink would have diminished and the likelihood of absenteeism decreased. Friday payment became widespread in some areas, notably in the west, but elsewhere these schemes seem to have backfired

113

as often as they succeeded.[43] Many of the innovators reverted to Saturday payment after discovering that payment during the week only facilitated longer drinking sprees by some workers. This was the complaint of the factory inspector in Elbing, West Prussia, who had convinced the industrialists in his district to abandon the traditional Saturday payment. The results were disappointing. 'The attempts to make wage payments on Friday', he observed, 'have been successful in only a few plants in which mostly females are employed.' 'Most factories', he continued, 'very quickly reintroduced Saturday as the payday since otherwise many people were fit for work neither on Saturday nor on Monday.'[44] With Saturday payments, on the other hand, absenteeism was at least confined to Mondays. Customary patterns of sociability thus died hard. Alone, the efforts of employers could do little to alter them.

But there were signs by the early twentieth century that popular drinking behaviour was changing. This was true not only on the job. Indeed changes in the use of alcohol at the workplace were clearly linked to broader changes in working-class drinking behaviour which were becoming increasingly evident after the turn of the century. The reasons for these broader changes, which reversed the long-term trend of rising per capita alcohol consumption characteristic of most of the nineteenth century, are difficult to determine with precision.[45] A number of factors were certainly at work, most of them gradual and cumulative in their effects. Better diet, shorter hours and new recreations helped make the use of alcohol less pressing, while a wide array of increasingly attractive consumer goods began to compete successfully for working-class purchasing power. But these factors, important as they are, do not explain why alcohol consumption declined when it did. This timing can best be understood as a product of rising living costs (including the costs of alcoholic beverages) and the slowed advance of real wages after the turn of the century.[46] In the face of this budgetary pressure many workers apparently curtailed their drinking in order to advance or defend their living standards in other areas. This is not to say that there was a massive conversion to teetotalism, but it does appear that large numbers of working men reduced their daily alcohol consumption in response to these budgetary pressures, especially, if not exclusively, on the job, where cheap alternative beverages were now increasingly available.

But this adjustment depended as much on new attitudes to alcoholic beverages as it did on the availability of suitable alternatives. The view that alcohol was an essential element of the working man's diet, a quasi-medicinal prophylactic against insalubrious working conditions and an indispensable ingredient of genuine manliness, was giving way to an ideal of moderate social drinking tolerant even of the abstainer. This new view was propagated not only by the public schools, the army and navy, the churches, the medical profession, bourgeois social reform movements and industrial employers, but also – and perhaps most successfully – by the organs of the German labour movement.

Recognizing the hygienic and financial advantages of reduced alcohol consumption as well as the importance of sobriety to occupational safety, trade unions and other organization of the labour movement worked actively from the turn of the century to alter working-class drinking behaviour.[47] They used their meetings and the columns of their press to educate workers about the true properties of alcohol and to encourage them to curtail their alcohol consumption, especially on the job. Though Christian trade unions more fully echoed the point of view of employers in blaming industrial accidents and inadequate living standards on immoderate drinking, the socialist Free Trade Unions also used their influence to combat on-the-job drinking and to reduce alcohol consumption generally. They fought artisanal drinking customs like *Einstand*[h] and the observance of *Blaue Montag*[i] and, knowing that heavy drinking only gave employers an excuse to keep wages low, occasionally even took the initiative in seeing that alcohol was banned from the workplace.[48] By justifying moderation to workers in terms that spoke directly to their needs and experiences and by using the prestige of the working-class press to dispel prevailing myths about alcohol's medicinal and nutritive properties, trade unions contributed significantly to the reduction of working-class alcohol consumption.

The success of these efforts was noted in a variety of factory inspectorate reports. In Minden, Westphalia, for example, the 1911 report concluded that it was due to the influence of the woodworkers' union (*Holzarbeiterverband*) in Bielefeld 'that its

115

members, among whom *Schnaps* consumption already has no place, are now also limiting their beer drinking during breaks and, especially in the morning, increasingly prefer milk as a beverage'.[49] This choice would have been virtually unthinkable two decades earlier. Many labour leaders agreed with this assessment of their union's influence in reducing popular alcohol consumption.[50] The propaganda of labour organizations and the example of their adherents, moreover, had an impact beyond the rather narrow confines of their formal membership. As a factory inspector in Württemberg discovered, the organizations of the labour movement set standards of behaviour that were widely emulated in the areas where they were prominent. 'In those cities', he reported, 'in which workers' organizations set the tone, complaints on the part of employers about drunkenness and the observance of Saint Monday are seldom heard.'[51]

A special survey conducted by the Prussian factory inspectors in 1907 revealed that with but few exceptions alcohol consumption had ceased to be a major problem for German industry.[52] Only in a few of Germany's technologically most primitive industries and economically most backward areas was the troublesome drinking of the past still widespread, perhaps because living standards there were especially low, the labour movement weak and the workforce particularly close to its largely rural and pre-industrial origins. Both Stehr's 1903 study and the survey of 1907 revealed that it was in the east – particularly in East and West Prussia and Silesia – that workers defended traditional drinking habits most tenaciously and that employers were most cautious in attempting to alter them.[53] Occupations little affected by mechanization and the factory system of production also continued to be plagued by heavy alcohol consumption. From all over Germany came reports of the disruptive drinking of stone-cutters, brick-makers, construction and cement workers; yet even in these occupations some improvement was noted in the years just preceding the war, at least in Germany's most thoroughly industrialized western regions.

Drinking thus remained a source of concern to German employers after the turn of the century, but the dimensions of the drink problem at the workplace had changed considerably in the decades before 1914. Drinking had ceased to be a problem of working-class culture and had become a problem of individual workers. The range of socially acceptable drinking styles had been broadened in the direction of greater moderation. Workers were 'no longer afraid', as a factory inspector in Hanover reported, 'to drink milk, coffee or tea in their pauses instead of beer or *Schnaps*'.[54] Forms of alcohol use that a decade or two earlier had seemed self-evident were now by and large abandoned and appeared in retrospect as the products of ignorance and poverty. Alcohol continued to play residual roles on the job and in the diet, but its use was becoming more and more exclusively a social activity, an accompaniment of almost all of the working-man's organized leisure activities. In Baden, for example, where factory inspectors had a long tradition of concern with the Drink Question, the report for 1913 concluded that 'the powerful temperance movement of the last decade has brought such enlightenment to working class circles that it is no longer possible to speak of alcohol abuse in Baden's working class; exceptions only prove the rule'.[55]

The changes in popular drinking behaviour noted by contemporaries were not due solely to the efforts of employers to discipline their workers. On their own, employers could no doubt impede the use of alcohol on the job, but it was only after workers themselves, often under the influence of their organizations, had discovered financial, hygienic and even political reasons of their own to curtail their alcohol consumption that drinking on the job ceased to be a pervasive and, for many employers and labour leaders alike, troubling aspect of German industrial life. In some areas of Germany and in some sectors of the economy, workers had not yet made this discovery by 1914.

What does the study of the Drink Question on the job tell us about the history of labour relations as Germany industrialized? In the first place, the persistence of drinking as a medium of social exchange on the job suggests that the workplace remained, even under the harshest conditions of early industrialization, the setting of multidimensional social interactions. The frequently posited dissociation of work from the other spheres of human experience, thought to have characterized the industrial mode of production from its inception, has obscured the extent to which the early factory system was an organizational rather than a technological innovation that permitted significant continuities in the work experience. Despite the formal demands made by employers on the new industrial labour force, the worker was not reduced to the proverbial cog in the great wheel of industry. The human material would not permit and the industrial situation did not demand such a transformation.[56] Workers brought with them inchoate conceptions, which they were willing to defend, of what labour relations should be like, and the production process in most industries was such that opportunities for conversation and conviviality remained.[57] Except perhaps in the most highly mechanized branches of textile production, industrialization in its early phases did not so much bring ceaseless attendance to a dehumanizing machine as it did the concentration of the factors of production, including labour power. It could indeed be argued that by bringing together a heterogeneous workforce of various skills and backgrounds, industrialization actually enhanced the social dimension of work. In any case, the persistence of forms of convivial drinking on the job is one piece of evidence that suggests that workers created and maintained a significant amount of social space at the work place. As Rudolf Braun has written of factory life in Canton Zürich, 'despite the restrictions of factory regulations, industrial noise and demands for performance . . . sociability could not be suppressed on the job'.[58]

Although both the social and physiological uses of alcohol on the job ultimately declined, the persistence of this kind of drinking into the early twentieth century, despite the efforts of industrialists to curtail it, is an important indication of the limits of the power of employers to discipline their workforce. Work discipline was a goal never perfectly realized. The rationally calculating employer was often forced to conclude that it was wiser to risk the disruption and inefficiency associated with alcohol consumption than to face the greater evils of collective resistance, epidemic job changing or shortfalls in the recruitment of labour. The protracted, if usually mute, struggles over the use of alcohol on the job suggest that workers, collectively if not individually, exercised considerably more control over what went on at the workplace than has commonly been supposed. At the very least, as Lawrence Schofer has recently argued, nineteenth-century labour relations on the factory floor must be conceived as a process of mutual accommodation.[59] Even before the intervention of trade unions, employers were forced to reckon with – and often to accede to – their workers' demands, expressed in persistent patterns of behaviour and based in long-standing cultural traditions.

Trade unions and other institutions of the labour movement had reasons of their own for taking up the Drink Question, and this was crucial to the ultimate success of efforts to curtail drinking on the job. Whether socialist or non-socialist, they were influential in reducing working-class alcohol consumption and inducing compliance with standards of conduct conducive at once to greater industrial efficiency and to the individual and collective advancement of the working class. It was a measure of their integration into the system of production under industrial capitalism that they combated artisanal drinking customs and encouraged sobriety both on the job and off. They hoped thereby to reap a greater share of the benefits created by a more productive organization of labour. But at the same time it should be clear that those within the labour movement who devoted their talents and energies to the fight against alcohol were not simply doing their masters' bidding. On the contrary, they believed they were providing workers not only with a means to cope better with their mundane daily problems but also – at least in the case of the socialists – with an important weapon in the class struggle. Temperance may have been a way of domesticating the working class in the minds of many employers and temperance reformers but for many members of the labour movement, it had a different meaning: it was a means to more pressing and often more radical ends. As Eric Hobsbawm has observed, the 'line between personal and collective improvement, between imitating the middle class and, as it were defeating it with its own weapons' was an extremely thin one in the nineteenth-century working class.[60]

EDITOR'S NOTES

a A strong alcholic drink.
b Workers were compelled to buy goods in the store run by their employer.
c An inexpensive but strong alcoholic drink.

d An enterprise making railroad equipment.
e Roughly, 1850–73.
f An administrative district.
g Craftsmen traditionally refrained from working on Mondays. Their customs sanctified Monday as a day of relaxation.
h As mentioned above, the customary obligation imposed on new workers to buy rounds of drinks for his comrades.
i Saint Monday.

NOTES

Journal of Social History 15 (Autumn 1981): 25–38. Reprinted with the permission of the *Journal of Social History*.

1 Sidney Pollard, *The Genesis of Modern Management: A Study of the Industrial Revolution in Great Britain* (Cambridge, Mass., 1965): 181–91; and E. P. Thompson, 'Time, work discipline and industrial capitalism', *Past and Present*, 38 (1967): 56–97. For Germany in particular, see: Jürgen Kocka, *Unternehmensverwaltung und Angestelltenschaft am Beispiel Siemens, 1847–1916*, Industrielle Welt, 11 (Stuttgart, 1969): 111–16, 213–16; J. J. Lee, 'Labour in German industrialisation', in Peter Mathias and M. M. Postan (eds), *The Cambridge Economic History of Europe* (Cambridge, 1978), vol. 7, part 1: 442–91; Lawrence Schofer, *The Formation of a Modern Labor Force: Upper Silesia, 1865–1914* (Berkeley, Calif., 1975): 121–37. For useful discussions of drink and industrial work discipline elsewhere, see: Brian Harrison, *Drink and the Victorians: The Temperance Question in England, 1815–1872* (Pittsburgh, PA, 1971): 40–1; and W. R. Lambert, 'Drink and work-discipline in industrial South Wales, c. 1800–1914', *Welsh History Review*, 7 (1975): 289–306.
2 Wolfgang Nahrstedt, *Die Entstehung der Freizeit* (Göttingen, 1972): 130, 222. cf. the words of caution in Lee, 'Labour in German industrialization': 466–8.
3 Ernst Engel, *Die Branntweinbrennerei in ihren Beziehungen zur Landwirtschaft, zur Steuer und zum öffentlichen Leben* (Dresden, 1853): 164; Theodor Laves, 'Die Entwicklung der Branntweinproduktion und die Branntweinbesteuerung in Deutschland', *Jahrbuch für Gesetzgebung, Verwaltung und Volkswirtschaft im Deutschen Reich*, 11 (1887): 1274–85.
4 Whether or not alcohol was in fact physiologically useful on the job, many workers believed that it was and justified their drinking accordingly. I have argued elsewhere that alcohol could provide useful calories on the job but that its precise effects depended on the nutritional status of each individual. See 'Drink and working class living standards in late 19th century Germany', in Werner Conze and Ulrich Engelhardt (eds), *Arbeiterexistenz im 19 Jahrhundert. Lebensgestaltung deutscher Arbieter und Handwerker* (Stuttgart, 1981).

5 A. H. Stehr, *Alkoholgenuss und wirtschaftliche Arbeit* (Jena, 1903): 44–6. See also, Otto Rühle, *Illustrierte Kultur- und Sittengeschichte des Proletariats*, 2 vols (Berlin, 1930; reprinted Frankfurt, 1971 and Lahn-Giessen, 1977), 1: 412–13; B. Laquer, 'Einfluss der sozialen Lage auf den Alkoholismus', in M. Mosse and G. Tugendreich (eds), *Krankheit und soziale Lage* (Munich, 1913): 473–95, here 482.

6 Rudolf Braun, *Industrialisierung und Volksleben*, vol. 2, *Sozialer und kultureller Wandel in einem ländlichen Industriegebiet (Zürcher Oberland) unter Einwirkung des Maschinen- und Fabrikwesens im 19. und 20. Jahrundert* (Erlenbach-Zurich, 1965): 211.

7 The association of skilled and relatively well-paid workers with heavy alcohol consumption has also been noted elsewhere. See E. A. Dingle, 'Drink and working-class living standards in Britain, 1870–1914', *Economic History Review*, 2nd series, 25 (1972): 608–22, here 618; Georges Duveau, *La Vie Ouvrière en France sous le Second Empire*, 4th edn (Paris, 1946): 498–522.

8 Wilhelm Bode, *Arbeiterschutz gegen den Alkohol* (Berlin, 1898): 2–3.

9 Emanuel Wurm, *Die Alkoholgefahr, ihre Ursachen und ihre Bekämpfung* (Hamburg, 1912): 114.

10 Reichsamt des Innern, *Jahresberichte der Gewerbeaufsichtsbeamten und Bergbehörden* (hereafter *Jahresberichte*), 1 (1904): 390; cf. Stehr, *Alkoholgenuss*: 26; Deutscher Verein gegen den Missbrauch geistiger Getränke, *Weitere Mitteilungen zum Kapitel 'Arbeiterschutz gegen den Missbrauch geistiger Getränke'* (Hildesheim, 1897): 6–7.

11 Reichsamt des Innern, *Amtliche Mitteilungen aus den Jahresberichten der mit Beaufsichtigung der Fabriken betrauten Beamten* (hereafter *Mitteilungen*) (1890): 226.

12 Stehr, *Alkoholgenuss*: 67–8; Rühle, *Illustrierte*: 414–20; Alfred Grotjahn, *Alkohol und Arbeitsstätte* (Berlin, 1903): 25–6.

13 H. von Glümer, *Schutz der Arbeiter gegen den Alkoholmissbrauch* (Hildesheim, 1897): 3.

14 Günter Anton, *Geschichte der preussischen Fabrikgesetzgebung*, Staats- und Sozialwissenschaftliche Forschungen, 12, part 2 (Leipzig, 1891): 152; Bode, *Arbeitershutz*: 28; J. H. Böttcher, *Uber den Branntwein-Genuss* (Hanover, 1839): 40; L. A. LaRoche (ed.), *Die Branntweinschrecknisse des neunzehnten Jahrhunderts* (Posen, 1845): 110–13, 272–3, 286–7; Carl Rösch, 'Ueber den Missbrauch geistiger Getränke', *Deutsche-Vierteljahrs-Schrift*, 1 (1838): 297.

15 'Die Enthaltsamkeitssache in der Rheinprovinz', *Beilage des Rheinischen Beobachters*, 283 (10 October 1845) (in Hauptstaatsarchiv Düsseldorf, Reg. Aachen 4793).

16 *Handwörterbuch der Staatswissenschaften*, 3rd edn., s.v. 'Trucksystem', by Wilhelm Stieda: 1267, 1271–2; Anton, *Geschichte*: 152; Grotjahn, *Alkohol*: 88–9; Stehr, *Alkoholgenuss*: pp. 70–6.

17 The provision of spirits to manual workers appears to have been a common practice in early phases of industrial development elsewhere as well. See, Harrison, *Drink and the Victorians*: 39; and John Allen Krout, *The Origins of Prohibition* (New York, 1925): 79.

18 LaRoche, *Die Branntweinschrecknisse*: 112.

121

19 Jürgen Kocka, 'Industrielles management: konzeption und modelle in Deutschland vor 1914', *Vierteljahrschrift für Sozial- und Wirtschaftsgeschichte*, 56 (1969): 332–72; Schofer, *Formation*: 145–6.
20 Böhmert's address, supplemented by further surveys, was later published. See, Victor Böhmert, *Der Branntwein in Fabriken*, neue Bearbeitung, Volkswohl-Schriften, 7 (Leipzig, 1889): here 12.
21 ibid.
22 The image of the carrot and the stick is borrowed from Pollard, *Genesis*: 126.
23 Wolfgang Krabbe, *Gesellschaftsveränderung durch Lebensreform: Strukturmerkmale einer sozialreformischen Bewegung im Deutschland der Industrialisierungsperiode* (Göttingen, 1974): 120–2.
24 *Jahresberichte*, 1 (1904): 373–4.
25 Grotjahn, *Alkohol*: 46–50; Stehr, *Alkoholgenuss*: 36–44 passim. Numerous examples are also cited in the reports of the factory inspectors.
26 Quoted in Bode, *Arbeiterschutz*: 1–2.
27 For examples of work stoppages in response to efforts by employers to regulate drinking behaviour, see, *Jahresberichte*, 1 (1901): 23; 1 (1905): 65; 1 (1906): 118–19, 212–13; 2, part 2 (1907): 370; 1 (1908): 51; Stehr, *Alkoholgenuss*: 27, 103–4.
28 Böhmert, *Der Branntwein*: 13.
29 Stehr, *Alkoholgenuss*: 63–4.
30 The relationship between work discipline and fluctuations in the labour market is also noted by Schofer, *Formation*: 81, 111, 135, 157–8; and Pollard, *Genesis*: 187.
31 Bode, *Arbeiterschutz*: 1–2. See also, *Jahresberichte*, 1 (1901): 98; 3, part 11 (1907): 18; Stehr, *Alkoholgenuss*: 26; Deutscher Verein gegen den Missbrauch geistiger Getränke, *Weitere Mitteilungen*: 6–7.
32 *Jahresberichte*, 3, part 26 (1901): 21. See also Stehr, *Alkoholgenuss*: 63–4.
33 Stehr, *Alkoholgenuss*: 64.
34 *Jahresberichte*, 1 (1901): 414; See also Stehr, *Alkoholgenuss*: 31.
35 Böhmert, *Der Branntwein*: 42–5; Deutscher Verein gegen den Missbrauch geistiger Getränke, *Weitere Mitteilungen*: 11–12.
36 W. Böhmert, 'Die Gast- und Schankwirtschaften, nebst Angaben über die polizeiliche Regelung des Wirtschaftsbetriebes und über die alkoholgegnerischen Vereine', *Statistisches Jahrbuch Deutscher Städte*, 29 (1913): 13–42; Olhausen, 'Die Frühpolizeistunde im Deutschen Reich', *Jahrbuch für Gesetzgebung, Verwaltung und Volkswirtschaft im Deutschen Reich* (1906): 845–82; Christian Stubbe, *Der deutsche Verein gegen den Missbrauch geistiger Getränke, 1883–1908* (Berlin, 1908): 27–30.
37 *Mitteilungen* (1876): 265–6.
38 *Jahresberichte*, 3, part 24 (1902): 19–20; 1 (1907): 126.
39 ibid., 1 (1901): 444.
40 ibid., 1 (1901): 429.
41 ibid., 1 (1901): 439. See also for the mining district of Diedenhofen in Alsace-Lorraine: 3, part 26 (1903): 83–4.

42 ibid., 1 (1902): 159; 1 (1903): 76–7; 1 (1909): 24–5; Schofer, *Formation*: 144–5.
43 For examples, see, *Mitteilhungen* (1894): 245–6; (1897): 81–3; (1898): 143; *Jahresberichte*, 2 (1899): 763; 1 (1909): 450–1.
44 *Jahresberichte*, 1 (1900): 18.
45 The quantity of absolute alcohol consumed in the forms of beer and spirits declined by 24 per cent between 1900 and 1913, from 9.1 litres per capita to 6.9. (Calculated from Walter G. Hoffmann, *Das Wachstum der deutschen Wirtschaft seit der Mitte des 19. Jahrunderts* (Berlin, 1965): 172–4, 651–2.) The explanation offered here of the decline of popular alcohol consumption in the early twentieth century is developed in greater detail in the author's 'Der Alkoholkonsum deutscher Arbeiter im 19. Jahrhunder', *Geschichte und Gesellschaft*, 6 (1980): 220–42.
46 The development of real wages after the mid-1890s remains a subject of controversy. There does, however, seem to be general agreement that real wages continued to rise in the early part of the twentieth century but at a much slower rate than in the period 1873 to 1896. Despite the continued – if considerably slowed – advance in real wages, however, there was a widely articulated sense among the working-class's spokesmen that wages were not keeping pace with rising living costs. This subjective sense of narrowing financial straits is more important to the argument being advanced here than the actual movement of real wages since it is this subjective sense that would have impelled workers to alter their choices as consumers. For a summary of recent findings on the question of real wages in this period, see Lees 'Labour in German industrialization': 471–73.
47 This was noted explicitly by factory inspectors in a variety of areas. See, for example, for Württemberg: *Jahresberichte*, 2, part 4 (1900): 75; 2, part 4 (1903): 81, 113; 2, part 4 (1908): 47–8; and for the Breslau district: 1 (1900): 93; 1 (1907): 65–6.
48 Illuminating information on the anti-alcohol activities of the Free Trade Unions is contained in 'Arbeiter und Alkoholkonsum', *Der Abstinente Arbeiter*, 5 (1907): 157–9, 165–6, 170–2. See also, the author's 'Drink and the labour movement: the *Schnaps* boycott of 1909', in Richard J. Evans (ed.), *The German Working Class: The Politics of Everyday Life* (London, 1981).
49 *Jahresberichte*, 1 (1907): 407.
50 'Arbeiter und Alkoholkonsum', *passim*.
51 *Jahresberichte*, 2, part 4 (1903): 113; cf. 'Arbeiter und Alkoholkonsum', 171.
52 *Jahresberichte*, 1 (1907): 11–12, 23, 34–5, 45–6, 64–6, 79–80, 105–7, 118, 126, 132–3, 148–50, 165–6, 176–8, 201–3, 213–16, 228–30, 239–42, 254–6, 266–8, 298–300, 313–14, 228–9, 361–3, 379–80, 398–9, 407–8, 439–42, 467–71, 488, 500–1.
53 ibid., 1 (1907): 11–12, 34–5, 45–6, 126, 148–50, 201–3; Stehr, *Alkoholgenuss*: 40.
54 *Jahresberichte*, 1 (1907): 286–8.

55 ibid., 2, part 5 (1913): 52.
56 For a similar conclusion based on somewhat broader consider-ations, see, Lee, 'Labour in German industrialization': 460–71 *passim.*
57 For useful insights into the work experience in a large industrial enterprise in the early 1890s, see, Paul Göhre, *Drei Monate Fabrikar-beiter und Handwerksbursche* (Leipzig, 1891): 40–88 *passim.*
58 Braun, *Industrialisierung*: 218.
59 Schofer, *Formation*: 138.
60 Eric Hobsbawm, *The Age of Capital, 1848–1875* (London, 1975): 226–7.

Part III

THE MAKING OF A
WORKING CLASS

It should be evident by now that proletarianization, the processes evoked by Tilly and Johnson, has been the major conceptual breakthrough of the new labour history. It seems to describe the experiences of ordinary people better than the Industrial Revolution paradigm. Moreover, it seems to explain why artisans came to identify themselves as 'workers' and built large labour movements. In short, social historians are very much inclined to link proletarianization and the rise of the working class.

However, Cannadine's essay demonstrates that reinterpretations are, for the most part, just a matter of time. Already in 1975, Peter Stearns's empirical analysis showed just how complicated were the connections between work experience, on the one hand, and the building of a labour movement, on the other hand. Applying more theoretical perspectives to the problem, William Sewell and Joan Scott now argue that the proletarianization model is not adequate for explaining how workers were radicalized or how they came to think of themselves as a class. Perhaps the critiques are a sign that the first 'generation' of social history is giving way to a second generation. Certainly, the political and social climate has evolved markedly since the new labour history emerged in the 1960s. A populist, anti-authoritarian impulse born of protest against the Vietnam War, the civil rights movement, aggressive welfare statism and anti-colonial struggles gave impetus to the new labour history. Today, scholars in that field must write in the context of failed revolution and reform. The anaemic situation of labour movements worldwide, the repudiation of communism, the vanquishing of socialist ideologies, and the prominence of women's struggles for full rights might well be leading to new historical interpretations. A future Cannadine might someday write 'The present and past of social history, 1960–2000'.

Be that as it may, the critics of proletarianization have a distinctive and interesting point of view. They are posing fundamental challenges to conventional modes of thinking about the past – and the present.

7

THE LIMITS OF LABOUR PROTEST

Peter N. Stearns

Around 1800, the strike was a rare occurrence. By 1900, it had become commonplace. The leading industrial countries of Europe had developed large working-class political parties by then, too. Whilst it would be tempting to tie the mass labour movements to widespread proletarianization, Peter Stearns shows that there were many intervening forces.

Stearns uses strike data from France, Britain, Belgium and Germany to gauge the attitudes of wage-earners towards their work and their lives. Beyond recognizing that most labourers suffered painful changes on the job, Stearns is reluctant to generalize. Some workers, he finds, received compensation in terms of better pay or more leisure. Still others bore their discontents in silence. Stearns believes that the strike data show the absence of a 'protest culture' among labourers. Even the most aggrieved failed to find ways to express – still less to redress – what bothered them most.

Readers will have to decide whether they accept the conclusions Stearns draws from the strike profiles. In any case, the points he emphasizes, the incompleteness of labour mobilization and the diversity of workers' experiences, have recently moved to the centre of scholarly concern. The final two readings approach these issues with new conceptual tools.

* * *

Substantial changes in work plus the limitations in developing compensations off the job explain much of the tide of protest that developed after 1890, a protest that had important precedents in earlier decades but which assumed massive and regular proportions in this period. The protest did not necessarily stem from rising discontent. . . . The protest of this period resulted partly from the availability of regular leadership and organization; workers in earlier stages of industrialization might have done as much or more, had these been at hand, just as their counterparts in Russia and Italy were attempting in these very years. But protest in western Europe had much to do with the changing work experience, and without surveying protest movements in great detail we must ask what the links were.

Unfortunately, protest did not develop in a predictably close relationship to problems on the job. While recognizing the extensive unrest of the period and the deep roots that protest organizations were taking within the working class, we must emerge with an impression of its tangential bearing on the work question. Put simply, protest did not directly convey the most basic complaints workers had about their jobs or the anguish that some of them felt at work. There were good reasons for this, which we will explore, but the gap between what might have been sought and what was sought remained potentially tragic. . . .

It can readily be agreed that strikes and some trade union activities constituted the most direct means of protest against job grievances. There is evidence in France as well as Britain that many workers turned to political remedies in this period only when prevented from striking or taught that strikes were ineffective.[1] While a comparable situation did not prevail widely in Belgium or Germany, given the chronological precedence of a mass socialist movement, here too strikes offer the most direct insight into the relationship between protest and work.

We touch, obviously, on a vast problem. Working-class protest had many sources beyond the work situation and, in focusing on the narrower relationship to the job, we do not pretend a complete assessment. Strikes alone offer a host of problems of interpretation. Their goals, which constitute our principal concern, are difficult to interpret. Many strikes began on an intensely personal note, only to convert to a general issue such as wages, at which point the government or union statistician duly recorded the effort. The smaller strikes, particularly, could reflect an even more complicated link with the job. Hastily-called strikes not infrequently conveyed a mixture of anger and pleasure, because they followed from the irregular work patterns which many workers sought to perpetuate. A textile strike in Ghent was voted, in a tumultuous meeting, mainly by young workers who thought the walk-out would be fun and wanted some free time for recreation. The effort was serious – focusing, appropriately, on a reduction of hours – but the atmosphere of celebration was important in itself. The same vacation air was noted in the massive Verviers[a] strike and often elsewhere. Quite apart from victory or defeat, strikes might relieve tensions at work by restoring a sense of control over its rhythms – and thus inhibit more far-reaching goals and efforts.[2]

The statistical problems in the assessment of strikes are formidable enough. . . . Comparisons across national boundaries are particularly chancy; trends within countries, over time, and inter-industry comparisons are far sounder. British records did not cover one-day strikes or movements with less than ten workers, which magnifies the average strike size reported but lowers the total of strikers. British statisticians, scrupulously honest, often could not determine the demand involved – hence percentages per demand often add up to less than 100. But they did insist in identifying only one demand, whereas German records listed multiple goals. Belgian records omitted political strikes, thus missing the two main efforts on the period; the Belgian strike rate is thus artificially low. Continental governments may also have underplayed goals such as union recognition, that had political overtones; the French and Belgian records seem wanting here. Germany was more honest, for government records and those provided by unions largely coincide on this point, and the unions admitted that most organizational goals really constituted the barest effort to keep union members from being dismissed. Britain, on the other hand, seemed bent on finding union recognition an issue wherever possible, doubtless because of the Board of Trade's desire to encourage responsible unionism as part of collective bargaining. . . .

Even the judgement of overall rates is complicated. A study of French strikes has claimed, plausibly enough, that the state missed about 10 per cent of all efforts. The number of strikers is of more concern here, because the interest is not in the strike as protest form or political event but as a reflection of workers' intent. Here the figures utilized probably distort in the other direction, because they convey peak numbers rather than the average through the strike. The problem of lockouts is thorny. The word is ominous, but lockouts were often little different from strikes, in terms of issues involved; many strikes, for their part, were actually triggered by employers. German figures show that lockouts were artisanal more than industrial, though important in machine building. If included they would raise the average strike rate by 32 per cent – making German figures more comparable with English and French – and they would change the pattern of issues involved, particularly by heightening conflicts over pay cuts and reducing the percentage of efforts over wages and particularly hours – all in keeping with figures from the other continental countries. . . .

The strike data unanimously point to one vital set of conclusions: workers struck rarely over job conditions, at least in any explicit way; such strikes were comparatively unsophisticated,[3] and relatedly such strikes tended to decrease with time. The first point is obvious enough. Nowhere did strikes over work conditions command more than a quarter of all strikers, and except for Belgium the figure was much lower; even in Germany, where the union statisticians disputed the government data, the rate was only 15 per cent (Table 7.1).

Normally also strikes over conditions were small (Belgium is again an exception); hence the strike rate was higher than

Table 7.1 Demand rate 1899–1917

| | % strikes per demand | | | % strikes per demand | | |
	France	Germany	Belgium	Britain	Germany	Belgium
Against cut	4.2	6.2	8.1	6.9	3.6	10.0
For raise	55.9	65.0	48.2	23.6	77.5	62.6
Total wage	63.0	71.2	56.3	58.5	84.1	72.6
Hours	15.5	32.4	6.6	5.8	55.9	9.0
Personal issues	24.3	20.9	22.1	6.0	16.8	10.8
Conditions	6.7	2.8	20.5	7.8	2.2	25.6
Union	3.5	6.1	2.9	18.2	34.1	1.3
Strike losses	41.6	41.5	58.2	24.1	35.5 (1907–13)	45.3

the striker rate. As a general rule, small strikes suggest a lack of general support for the issue involved and are tactically unwise: strikers are intensely and intelligently aggrieved, but they are in early stages of a strike movement. This judgement, admittedly debatable, finds some confirmation in the industries most concerned with conditions in their strikes. Transport workers predominated, and the reason for the high incidence of strikes over conditions in Belgium is the large Antwerp dock strike over hiring methods and work rules. Here was the statistical reflection of concern over changes in work organization and the growing desire for more stable employment. These strikes also expressed the desire for dignity and freedom which impressionistic materials from dockers and sailors convey more dramatically. But in the factories and among artisans whose units of employment were becoming larger, strikes over conditions were rare. . . .

Several factors progressively deterred strikes over conditions. First, these strikes were among the hardest to win; employer resistance was much keener here than in issues of hours or wages, in almost every industry and area. With growing experience in the strike movement, then, workers would learn to avoid these issues in favour of wage demands. Often a transition was made during a strike itself. In 1899 the London plasterers' union struck to force foremen into their union and to limit apprenticeship. Worker sentiment ran high. But the strike simply could not be won, and the workers' insistence on some positive gain turned to a raise, which was granted.[4] We can safely assume that far more strikers wanted to invoke job conditions than finally managed to do so, which is one reason that the strike movement inadequately conveyed work grievances. Yet a more permanent conversion to other kinds of issues can be traced in many cases, which accounts for the longer-term evolution of strike demands. Silesian[b] miners often protested work conditions in the 1890s. They were just beginning to face the new production levels and impersonal management that were increasingly a part of modern industry. Their strikes lost, and after a period of readjustment in which protest of any sort was low they re-emerged with well-organized strikes for wages and hours gains right before the War.[5] Relatedly, many workers were not overwhelmingly discontented with their work arrangements. The strike statistics tend to confirm the ambiguity about changes in technology and work systems that can be drawn from the direct study of work.

Yet obviously the problem does not end with this statement. The disparity between the laments of German workers about their job, . . . which Adolf Levenstein[c] recorded, and the low level of strikes suggests a real problem of translating grievances into strike goals, compounded obviously by the intense employer resistance. We can gain further insight into the disparity by examining another key category of strike demands, the protests for or against individuals. As we have seen, strikes against a hated foreman or director form an important part of the ongoing tensions on many job sites. Strikes against the dismissal of a worker for insufficient production were more common than protests against the work systems that sought to heighten production. The boundary line is not easy to draw, but the personal factor was important. It reflected the small-group loyalty that remained important even in the larger factories. German workers displayed attachment to their colleagues even in their styles of dress, speaking often of *Saalmoden*, or styles of the workroom. Skilled workers often did not know their fellows with different skills or in other divisions of the plant, so a general issue over work conditions or employer policy would make little sense. But an affront to someone they knew might bring them out quickly. . . .

If workers found it difficult to mount direct attacks on the quality of work itself, they were more successful in trying to win a reduction of work. The strike movement on the whole confirms the notion of an increasingly instrumental view of work, in which full pleasure in work was abandoned as unobtainable – at least by those workers who were aggrieved enough to strike at all – and better conditions off the job were sought in compensation. Strikes for a reduction of hours were consistently among the most highly sophisticated, as measured by their large average size and their generally good success rate. They had strong union backing, which both explains and reflects their tactical sophistication. . . . They loom large in mining generally, often in conjunction with legislation; hours strikes in British and Belgian mining around 1910 concerned more the implementation of shorter hours than the hours themselves, which explains why this was the only industry in which hours strikes clearly rose. Miners were, more than most others, concerned about limiting their work. Otherwise the groups most vigorously interested were those from a craft background, particularly printers and construction workers. This helps explain the high rate of hours strikes in Germany, for craftsmen played an unusually active role in strikes generally. Artisanal strikes reflect the new lifestyle that was being forged, in which leisure played an important role. Artisans also had a long tradition of seeking shorter hours to counter unemployment, and this visibly continued.

Finally, workers as a whole did not show a desire, through strikes at least, to press hours down indefinitely. On the Continent strikes over hours of work peaked in 1905–6, as printers countered technological change and as construction workers, emerging from a long slump, tried to fight unemployment. Thereafter they normally declined as other issues took the fore. The pattern is clearer still in Britain, where strikes to reduce hours loomed large in the 1890s but dropped considerably thereafter. Three factors limited hours as an issue of consistent interest, despite trade union promptings in this direction: legislation could be seen as more effective than strikes, though strike success rates were good, save in Germany; the fear of loss of pay was a consistent inhibition; and after a certain level was reached, usually 9 to 10 hours outside the mines, the desire for further gains was limited, at least when measured against other goals *and* when rates of unemployment declined (an obvious factor in the waning British rate). Obviously this does not coincide with what some labour leaders said or with the fervour with which some workers embraced 8 hours campaigns; it does coincide with what most workers expressed through their strikes. . . .

If one adds up the strikes over work and related conditions and over hours, considering their evolution over time and their industrial incidence, it is impossible not to conclude that striking workers were generally either satisfied with their jobs *per se*, or convinced that direct protest was less effective or desirable than a quest for better wages or incapable of translating the real grievances they felt into explicit strike goals. The fact that workers disagreed over such issues as the piece-rate – outside the crafts – was itself a major factor in limiting the frequency and sophistication of strikes over work. Protest remained, as it had traditionally been for the lower classes, an expression of problems as consumers.[d] Here was probably the most general reason for the apparent disparity between grievances and strikes. The form of protest had shifted, involving the workplace more commonly than the merchant, but the cast of mind had not. The poverty of many workers explains the wage focus in part, but the element of continuity with the older protest tradition should not be minimized. . . . [6]

The need to use protest as consumers, rather than in specific response to the work situation, was massively heightened by the inflation after 1900. More workers were ready to embrace a rising living standard than were able to do so once inflation hit; protest had increasingly to be reserved for defence of existing levels. Here was the main reason for the growing incidence of apparently offensive wage strikes. The great increase in German strikes by 1912–13 coincided with a peak in wage demands. The comparable, though far more pronounced, British crest in the same years has been subject to more varied if somewhat inconclusive interpretation. Part of the attention has resulted from the shock the strike wave caused British political and business leaders, a significant topic in itself. Some analysis has suggested incipient rebellion, and has invoked rising class consciousness and challenges to traditional skill status. But causal explanations, where they can be pinned down, must rely on the inflation-caused pressure on real wages above all.[7] And this is largely confirmed by actual strike demands. Wage demands were high in 1911 (particularly if the dockers' strike is given its due) and in 1913, and overwhelming in 1912. In clothing, engineering, mining and in fact in transport offensive wage demands rose in rate as well as in the absolute number of strikes they motivated, compared to the previous decade. . . .

The inflation did help teach new categories of workers to expect rising money wages – like the silk-workers of Voiron who could, after some strikes for raises to keep pace with prices, invoke 'our normal rising wage' by 1913[8] – and in the long run may have encouraged an instrumental approach to problems at work, at least in orienting strike goals away from work itself. For the pre-war period, apart from the small groups of workers whose real wages did rise, the actual framework for wage strikes leaves us with the familiar dilemma. In defending their living standards workers were not clearly converting to the kind of rising expectations that would compensate for new pressures at work and were not able massively to protest these new pressures directly.

Correspondingly there is no general relationship between pressures on the job, as perceivable through complaints of individual workers or examination of work systems themselves, and the strike rate in the major industries. Miners everywhere led the way, with a slight lag in Germany because of the presence of more new workers and firmer employer resistance. The dangers they faced and the organizational advantages offered by the mining villages account for their lead more than any major change in the nature of work, though more difficult conditions at the pit-face did play a role. After this statement, however, generalization becomes much more difficult. Transport workers demonstrated considerable relative activity in France and Britain, far less in Belgium and Germany; the variation was due less to conditions of work than recency of rural origin and levels of competition for jobs, on the docks, and the constraints and attractions of state versus private service, on the rails. Construction workers were active in France and Germany, sluggish in Belgium and Britain. Again, the distinction has less to do with job situation than with the vigour of the industry, the heavy rural base of Belgian workers and the fact that British unions had gained, during the 1890s, many of the goals that their French and German counterparts were later striving for. Textile workers struck with some frequency in France and Britain, rarely in Belgium and Germany; here job conditions may have played some role, as French and particularly British firms were technologically more advanced, but nowhere were strikes particularly common. Chemical workers struck rarely, and only over wages, yet their industry was changing rapidly and variations relate mainly to pressures on pay levels (as in France where legislated hours reduction caused most of the big strikes over wages). The case of metals and machinery is more anomalous still. Nowhere did the industry offer a per capita strike rate much above the national average and generally it was far lower than this. Here workers new to the industry, with craft expectations, may have been more vigorous in their complaints, for the French and German rates are higher than those in Belgium and Britain where the industry was older and speculations about the disruptive effects of new methods more common.

Employer resistance played some role in variations in strike rates. Everywhere metal and machine workers suffered higher strike losses than most other groups, which would have deterred them from further efforts. Yet strike loss was not always such a deterrent, as in the case of German and Belgian mining or the British transport group. More important were factors of residence and tradition which have been cited already. The role of the cohesion of mining villages and their proximity to work has often been discussed, for miners continue to lead the list of workers with a high propensity to strike. Maritime workers were beginning to make their claim to second place. But many artisans were placed higher than they are on a contemporary list (where printers and construction workers, for example, are listed in the medium rank).[9] Their position derives partly from the relative inactivity of factory workers, partly from the effort to establish new bargaining procedures to protect traditional job goals and gain new leisure and earnings for life off the job. Hence German printers had a high strike rate, though less pressed by new technology, while those in France and particular Britain and Belgium, with collective agreements more firmly established, were already in the medium to low range. And artisanal tradition seems to have played a role in those cases where rates of striking in machine industry were high.

Collectively, factory workers fall below the concentrated urban crafts (though not, of course, more traditional sectors such as food processing) in their strike rate. They were often still new to each other and residentially scattered, but the low strike rate of many British factory workers is a warning against pressing novelty too far. To be sure, where job changing was frequent it went hand in hand with rapid fluctuations in union membership – still rising annually in the German metalworkers' union in 1911, when 75 per cent of all new members left the union and 44 per cent of the total membership had joined only a year before.[10] But even in more settled cases, such as British engineering, the strike rate remained far lower than the grievances about innovations on the job suggest. For factory workers generally, as indeed for much of the working class, strikes were not primarily weapons against changes at work. Strike patterns in most of the factory industries reflect job problems in the slightly increased incidence of strikes over conditions and, especially, personal issues, but if these were the tip of an iceberg they were too unsophisticated, too personalized and too hard to win to bring much else to the surface. Strikes depended above all on the wage situation, and in wages many of the factory workers (in metals, though, more than in textiles) were comparatively well-off, in relation to their own past and to other groups of workers as well. Furthermore we must not minimize the extent to which factory workers had devised defences against the worst problems on the job or found means of enduring if not enjoying innovations. When a mere 0.4 per cent of all German strikes and lockouts occurred over resistance to overtime, for example, the impression that most workers either appreciated overtime or found means to avoid it grows stronger.

Overriding the issue of radically different strike rates is the fact that most workers did not strike at all in the fifteen years before the First World War. Simple arithmetic shows that over 5 per cent of the workforce had to strike annually, on the average, for even a bare majority to be involved. Coal-miners met this criterion easily; their strike rate was higher than gross juxtaposition with census figures indicates, for the latter include other excavating workers as well. But no other group did. Big-city construction workers probably did, but not construction workers overall. It has been easy to neglect or belittle the mass of workers who did not engage in direct-action protest; they have received almost no historical attention. And their position is not related to work alone; religious interest, proximity to the land, even family problems could keep them out of action. Distinctive work situations could play a role, however. Bakers who found traditional dependence on their masters acceptable (if only because they expected to rise to the superior position themselves) or clothing workers spread out in the countryside and happy that they could avoid factory work saw no reason to strike; hence the obviously low strike rates in clothing and food processing. But it would be simplistic to pass the statistical problem off as the result of backward, if large, pockets of traditional production forms. What of the chemical workers or that 60-plus per cent of all machine-builders or textile workers who did not strike? . . .

To explain differential strike rates and the much greater problem of non-striking, it is more useful to identify a few key types of workers, even without firm statistical precision, than to multiply fairly obvious descriptive categories. Some workers were held back from striking by repression. Others did not strike because they were satisfied, or had to strike only rarely to maintain their satisfaction. Still others might venture a strike but unsuccessfully, for they did not find *organized* protest relevant to their grievances at work. All of this, obviously, within a framework in which real wages, while not rising, were not falling much either and in which protest for most workers still depended on perceivable deterioration in consumption levels.

The satisfied workers were mainly skilled. They encompass many in the most traditional trades, such as the bakers already cited; neither radical (the French syndicalists) nor moderate unions could rouse many of these workers. They include key skilled groups within the factories. Clickers in the shoe industry joined unions only reluctantly, when mechanization began to change their work conditions; but they still regarded themselves as an elite and in union meetings objected to frequent use of the word 'strike'.[11] Smiths, in German metal and machine shops, were another stolid category, unusually stable and proud of their strength and skill. And while it is true that traditional sources of satisfaction were often being eroded, it would be wrong to expect quick or thorough conversion to a protest mood.

Shading off from non-protesters were groups who collectively were willing to strike but, after a period of adjustment on their part and their employers', simply did not need to very often. Here the printers and skilled construction workers serve as prime examples, but the pattern extends to brewers, many woodworkers and to specific skill groups even in the larger factories. Generally the artisanal tradition was crucial to this pattern of adaptation. Some workers saw no need to strike at all. Small-town construction workers, like those described in Hastings by Robert Tressell, found the very notion that they should be aggrieved offensive to their dignity as men. The tenacious idea of the free-born Englishman could be applied against protest as well as for it. But relatively low strike rates among artisans must be explained in large part by increasingly successful collective bargaining; this is why strike rates tended to fall in this group. A strike wave might be essential to establish the principle of bargaining, as in France and Germany around 1906. But job dissatisfaction was not intense and various means apart from protest were developed to preserve key job conditions. To protect these means in turn, and to keep wages up, bargaining was more important than strikes. . . .

There were satisfied workers in the factories too, and their impact should not be minimized. Special skills, the upgrading of many unskilled workers, the impact of paternalistic programmes which sometimes included grievance procedures more effective than those won by unions in these industries – a host of factors could disincline workers from the admittedly risky and costly business of striking. Two other factors were involved as well, however, affecting many types of workers but particularly those in the larger units, which returns us to the sense that many – though by no means all – workers suffered from a gap between outlets for direct protest and grievances on the job.

Many workers could not strike because of employer repression. Despite high levels of grievance coal-miners in isolated areas of southern France were blocked from striking after a few abortive efforts in the 1890s.[12] Miners in Montceau-les-Mines who rebelled against the dictatorship of a company town in 1899 had to hold off from strikes thereafter, though they remained unionized and voted socialist. The thousands of French metallurgical workers blacklisted in the period were another group that might have struck again if freer from employer domination. In the countless other cases workers could never even try to strike because of employer surveillance; we can only guess at their number. But gross repression has severe limitations as a general explanation of non-striking. Coal-miners who did strike faced most of the same employer barriers as metallurgists, which could, as we have seen, lead to a high rate of strike defeat; but their protest rate was consistently elevated. We must assume that factors other than repression were operative, and this is partly confirmed by the low strike rate of metallurgists even where, as in Britain, employer resistance was modest. In a similar if less dramatic comparative case, it would be tempting to assume that far more British engineers wanted to strike than could, given their many complaints about work changes, but were blocked by the adamant resistance of employers which had already led to the successful lockout of 1897–8. But why then not develop a strike rate at least equal to that of German machine workers, whose employers were fully as hostile as the British? Repression is by no means irrelevant as an explanatory factor. It can in fact be elaborated if we turn from exclusive focus on the large manufacturers. Small masters or individual foremen could hold workers back more directly than often ineffective employer associations. Worker hierarchies played a major role as well. Older textile workers often prevented the unionization of their aides. Unskilled metallurgical workers were inhibited by job insecurity and the active hostility of the skilled group, so that low strike rates in this industry reflected a combination of employer repression, worker division and inter-group repression and the positive satisfaction which most skilled workers gained from advancing technology and rising pay.

In additon to satisfaction and repression, the irrelevance of protest organization to many workers' grievances must be added in explaining the low strike rate. This was a theme echoed by female and male workers alike. Mechanics in the Paris region, quite ready to criticize factory conditions, refused to join the union, for they wanted no additional discipline and hoped to do as they pleased at least off the job. A British railway worker put the thought directly: unions 'take away manhood and bind us rigidly down'.[13] Some workers tried to strike without unions, particularly in France where radical syndicalist rhetoric added to the fears; only 73 per cent of all French strikes had any union members involved at all. A significant though smaller minority of German strikes were conducted on the same basis, and many factory workers joined unions just briefly for the strike itself; in German textiles, machines and mining an average of 47 per cent of unionized strikers had been members for less than six months (compared to 17 per cent in the craft industries, for the years 1901–14).[14] Predictably, however, strikes without unions were doomed to high rates of failure, so the widespread tension between the constraints of organization and many workers' protest goals more commonly inhibited any collective action. . . .

What the unions did not and perhaps could not do, due to their need to avoid too-frequent strikes and win the strikes they conducted in order to retain members, was develop a serious programme of demands relating to conditions on the job. They were vital to the working class, as rising membership levels attest, but mainly on the wage front. They reconciled the divisions among workers over the work experience by ignoring them as much as possible, through the universal solvent of wage demands and related benefits. Their policies, combined with the growing bureaucratization, to which many workers were keenly sensitive, could backfire. In Germany, as in England, the rising strike rate of the pre-war years had something to do with the disparity between union efforts and job changes, though inflation was the more general trigger. The British railway union found its members increasingly hard to control, while restiveness in the Welsh mines and among German shipbuilding workers was partly directed against labour leadership.[15] A German worker voiced the general complaint: 'What use is it for us to pay our dues but have nothing to say; pay and work time are set from above.'[16] Yet even these criticisms veiled the real tragedy. Workers could see that many aspects of their jobs had escaped their control. They might talk, as British railway workers did, of the inadequacy of grievance procedures and certainly of the excessive centralization of unions themselves. And it is possible, as historians have noted, to see the changes in work organization and challenges to traditional factory skills as a vital backdrop to the rising crest of strikes. But as a backdrop only; strike demands were little changed, save as they concentrated with increasing ferocity on the wage issue. . . .

For a variety of reasons, then, including workers' own internal divisions, the importance of other issues, employer resistance patterns and the impulses of labour leadership, a period that could have seen the development of durable guidelines for defending job satisfaction did not do so. Efforts at qualifying the employers' decision-making power were significant, and here the unions played a vital role. The beginnings of the shop-stewards' movement revealed considerable concern in several industries.[17] But this left the nature of work untouched except in individual factories, not a matter of general bargaining. One cannot escape the conclusion that workers as a whole were not sufficiently aggrieved about their jobs, at least in relation to other problems, to mount a major direct protest. This left those workers who were concerned tragically bereft of support. It deprived the labour movement of a potentially explosive issue, far more likely to rouse revolutionary ardour than wage demands or even many union recognition issues, because it might call the principles of industrial operation into question. Just as important it set a rather durable tone for the labour movement itself, in which individual job grievances might be handled but at the wider level the nature of work largely ignored in favour of pressure over wages and benefits off the job.

Strikes and unions do not form the whole protest story, of course. The socialist movement may have had a more direct relationship to work grievances than the incidence of strikes and strike demands. Socialist voting was less constrained by repression and less qualified, because of the periodic nature of politics, by the desire of many workers to avoid further organizational control. One could be a firm individualist but still usually vote socialist come election day. Rising levels of socialist voting could easily reflect rising concern about the quality of work, though of course many other issues were involved. Very impressionistic evidence suggests that the nature of socialist voting may have varied with the quality of work plus the availability of other relevant protest outlets. We would need precise correlations of voting levels with types of workers to advance this hypothesis firmly, and these may never be obtainable. There is certainly ample evidence that workers with strong unions and an abundant strike outlet were less likely than others to vote socialist or at least to see socialism as anything but an adjunct to bargaining efforts. Hence socialism was relatively weak in the French mines and of course in many British industries, while somewhat stronger in the German mines. The majority of Belgian miners were firmly socialist – rural migrants excepted – but their vision of socialist triumph, as expressed to journalists during the 1913 general strike, often consisted mainly of higher wages and shorter hours rather than a real revamping of the social structure. Textile workers, at the other extreme, were, outside of Britain, likely to be particularly fervent socialists, with the obvious exception that domestic manufacturers were rarely attracted at all. Guesdist doctrine[e] in France caught on most firmly among textile workers in factories in the Nord and other centres such as Roanne: 24 per cent of the party membership consisted of

textile workers, well above its share in the industrial population. German textiles provide a similar impression: more than
miners or metalworkers they talked to Levenstein of their
hopes for a future society, which predominated over any desire
to earn more money. These were workers quite likely to be
discontented with their jobs, without strong unions and without a clearly instrumental view of work in which striving for
higher pay might serve as a compensation. In contrast socialism among most metalworkers and artisans, though quite
probably more significant numerically, was taken somewhat
less seriously as a panacea for problems on the job. Many
artisans embraced socialism while hoping for their own bicycle
repair shop; this ambivalence may account, in France, for their
slighter percentage role among party membership. Metalworkers
talked of the desirability of socialist victory in qualifying the
employers' control over job conditions, but spoke also of the
irrelevance of much socialist doctrine and the inevitability of a
social hierarchy; this had something to do with their own
relatively high job satisfaction and their desire and ability to
command a rising wage. Straws in the wind, to be sure, but
the possibility of significant correlation between the intentions
behind a socialist commitment and conditions on the job
remains high.[18]

What did a fervent socialist commitment do for the admittedly uncountable number of workers profoundly alienated
from their jobs? In Germany the miner Max Lotz – he who
found himself so different from most of his fellows – gives us
one suggestion. He hated his work, finding it increasingly
degrading, and he specifically renounced the notion that any
wage could compensate for its horrors. 'Therefore I depend
with all my being on the courage and idealism of socialism.'[19]
A metalworker expressed a similar sentiment, when he said
that socialism 'made a man' of him, sustaining him whenever
he felt sad.[20] These were people who thought of socialism on
the job and oriented their whole lives around the movement.
Here, then, from a prosaic standpoint, was another way of
getting through life. Yet again, without challenging the vital
importance of socialism, we can ask about the implications for
work. These were people whose commitment actually turned
them away from specific suggestions about the job; they really
gave up any hope of pleasure in work for the present. It

diverted them also from instrumental demands, where job grievances could be translated into wage goals, and this may explain yet another group of workers unlikely to strike in several industries and countries. The point was to wait for the future. From a larger vantage point it has already been noted for German socialism, and could be for Belgian as well, that the network of socialist organizations, by filling the spare time of the most fervent socialists, distracted from direct-action protest, and particularly from protest relating to work. Finally, for those who were deeply involved in socialist activities, the socialist impulse, like the union impulse, directed attention to the virtues of good work, discipline and sobriety and may thus have contributed to the creation of a more assiduous workforce.[21]

The labour movement in most of its aspects – politics, organization and direct action – neither reflected nor promoted a massive, coherent demand for basic changes on the job. Had the socialist vision triumphed real reforms would have resulted; the workers' councils movements that burgeoned right after the First World War showed that the desire for new controls within industry had only increased. Even before the war the significance of the labour movement for many aspects of working-class life and its profound, increasingly upsetting impact on the ruling class need no qualification here. But from the standpoint of work itself, the clearest common denominator of the working class, there was a missed opportunity. Their organizational imperatives and, often, their middle-class training left many labour leaders incapable of understanding the job reactions of many aggrieved workers, while the latter were incapable of a very clear expression on their own account. The result was not, in the pre-war period itself, a *révolution manquée.*[f] Enough workers were satisfied with their jobs or capable of translating grievances into improvements in life off the job to blunt any job-based revolutionary effort. A minority was not being served, and this may have some bearing on the general minority–majority split within the labour movement that became increasingly visible as the war approached. Of more durable significance is the fact that the failure to develop a protest culture directed at work itself left a dubious legacy for the future. The labour movement was at this period in a formative stage and changes in jobs were extremely significant.

For many decades the labour movement would find it difficult to raise issues relating directly to life at work, and their silence pushed their constituents towards interests in wages or even job control that could easily let the quality of work itself slide. This could weaken the response of organized labour when job dissatisfactions did find expression, a problem apparently reviving in the 1970s. Still more important, it could encourage many workers to spend almost half their waking hours as adults in an endeavour which they found joyless and, still worse, expected to remain joyless and beyond control. Even for the workers less profoundly alienated and for those to whom the gains of the labour movement brought real satisfaction, the absence of a protest culture that could deal directly with job change could prove an ongoing disability.

EDITOR'S NOTES

a A Belgian industrial town.
b A province of Germany.
c A pioneering researcher on working-class life in Germany.
d Before the mid-nineteenth century, protests over food prices were the most common form of popular protest.
e The Marxian doctrines of Jules Guesde, which called for a centralized party to control trade-union activity.
f The revolution that did not happen.

NOTES

From Peter N. Stearns, *Lives of Labor: Work in Maturing Industrial Society* (New York, 1975): 300–31. Copyright © 1975 by Holmes & Meier Publishers, Inc. Reprinted by permission of the publisher. Ellipses are used at the request of the publisher.

1 Leo Loubère, 'Coal miners, labor relations, and politics in the Lower Languedoc', *Journal of Social History* vol. 2 (1968): *passim*; Harvey Mitchell and Peter N. Stearns, *Workers and Protest* (Itasca, Ill., 1971): *passim*.
2 G. C. Ruther, 'A Propos d'une interpellation de M. Anseele sur la grève cotonnière gantoise', *Revue sociale catholique* (1905–6): 65–8; Laurent Dechesne, *L'Avènement du régime syndical à Verviers* (Paris, 1908).
3 On assessing strike 'sophistication', admittedly a risky endeavour, see Peter N. Stearns, 'Measuring the evolution of strike movements', *International Review of Social History* vol. 19 (1974): 1–27;

Charles Tilly and Edward Shorter, 'The shape of strikes in France', *Comparative Studies in Society and History* vol. 13 (1971): 60–86.

4 Onlooker (A. H. Telling), *Hitherto* (London, 1930): 55.

5 Lawrence Schofer, 'Patterns of worker protest: Upper Silesea, 1865–1914', *Journal of Social History* vol. 5 (1972): 447–63.

6 George Rudé, *The Crowd in History* (New York, 1964); Stearns, 'Measuring': *passim*.

7 George Dangerfield, *The Strange Death of Liberal England* (New York, 1961): 214ff.; E. H. Phelps Brown, *Growth of British Industrial Relations* (London, 1959): *passim*; Standish Meacham, ' "The sense of an impending clash": English working-class unrest before the First World War', *American Historical Review* vol. 92 (1972): 1343–64. Two statistical points must be added to the British conundrum. If cross-national per capita comparisons even approximate reality, the British post–1909 rate, when amalgamated with the exceptionally low 1899–1909 rate, was largely a catch-up operation. And this rate, for groups like miners and transport workers, more definitely merely heightened 1890s rates in Britain, which means that the main interpretive problem is not post-1909 but 1899–1909. All of which reduces, perhaps, the revolutionary impact of post-1909, save possibly on a nervous British government.

8 Archives nationales (France) F⁷ 13868, report on Milhau glove workers.

9 Clark Kerr and Abraham Siegel, 'The interindustry propensity to strike', in A. Kornhaus *et al.* (eds), *Patterns of Industrial Conflict* (New York, 1954): 190ff. One recent study does claim that artisans, inside as well as outside of factories, led in pre-1914 strikes and that their strikes had a high job-issue content. French ribbon-weavers thus struck a bit more intensely than cotton-spinners, and invoked job issues three times as often. But the comparison does not hold overall. Even in textiles craft groups like cloth printers struck no more over job issues than spinners did; factory weavers, hardly artisans, struck more often than craft groups. The distinctions may work better in metals, where small-shop smiths and moulders outstripped less threatened groups like factory mechanics and electricians, but again without producing a high overall rate of job-issue strikes in the industry. Work is relevant to strikes, in other words, but not decisively so. The same study finds the primary correlations with strikes up to 1914 in trends of prices, wages and the like, so that while some conclusions differ those judgements of the present chapter and those of Edward Shorter and Charles Tilly that bear on specific groups of workers, especially for this pre-First World War period, might be deemed largely congruent. Edward Shorter and Charles Tilly, *Strikes in France, 1830–1968* (Cambridge, 1974): *passim*.

10 Der Deutsche Metallarbeiter-Verband, *Jahr- und Handbuch für Verbandsmitglieder* (1911) (Stuttgart, 1912).

11 Alan Fox, *A History of the National Union of Boot and Shoe Operatives* (Oxford, 1958): 136.

12 Loubère, 'Miners', *passim*.
13 G. W. Alcock, *Fifty Years of Railway Trade-unionism* (London, 1922): 435; see also Union corporative des ouvriers mécaniciens de la Seine, *Brochure de propagande* (Paris, 1908): 9.
14 'Tabellen' in Generalkommission der deutschen Gewerkschaften, *Correspondenzblatt*, 1904ff.
15 G. C. Halverson, *The Development of Labour Relations in the British Railways since 1860*, Ph.D thesis (University of London, 1952); Jakob Heinen, 'Die Organisationsform der Gewerkschaften', *Die Neue Zeit* (1913–14): 546–8.
16 Philipp A. Koller, *Das Massen- und Führer-Problem in der Freien Gewerkschaften* (Tubingen, 1920): 89.
17 Branko Pribićević, *The Shop Stewards Movement and Workers' Control* (Oxford, 1959).
18 Claude Willard, *Les Guesdistes* (Paris, 1965): *passim*; Adolf Levenstein, *Die Arbeiterfrage* (Munich, 1913): 235 and *passim*; Paul Göhre, *Drei Monate Fabrikarbeiter* (Leipzig, 1913): *passim*; Fritz Schumann, *Auslese und Anpassung der Arbeiterschaft in der Automobilindustrie* (Leipzig, 1911).
19 Levenstein, *Arbeiterfrage*: 69; see also Adolf Levenstein, *Aus der Tiefe, Arbeiterbriefe* (Berlin, 1908): *passim*.
20 Levenstein, *Arbeiterfrage*: 317.
21 Guenther Roth, *The Social Democrats in Imperial Germany* (Totowa, NJ, 1963): *passim*.

8

UNEVEN DEVELOPMENT, THE AUTONOMY OF POLITICS AND THE RADICALIZATION OF WORKERS

William H. Sewell, Jr

Replacing the Industrial Revolution with proletarianization as the fundamental social change may well represent an instance of intellectual progress. However, there is real danger of falling into a familiar trap. Proletarianization can be just as much a paradigm, with its own set of unquestioned assumptions, as the Industrial Revolution has been. Sewell asks historians to rethink the significance of the concept before it congeals into a problematical generalization. In truth, he is reiterating Johnson's overlooked plea to grasp 'the whole of working-class experience'.

Sewell does so by returning to Samuel's demonstration of uneven, multi-directional change. Sewell draws the implication that economic development produced both proletarianized workers and pockets of privileged workers. Working-class politics emerged from both groups, and perhaps most particularly from the second.

If proletarianization was not the universal, ubiquitous process labour historians have taken it to be, then the relation between work and protest needs re-examination. The link Johnson provides can only be part of the answer. Sewell uses the case of nineteenth-century dockworkers to expand the scope of analysis beyond proletarianization.

Sewell's conclusions about how the dockworkers were radicalized are controversial and stimulating, for they question basic modes of reasoning in labour history. Scholars in this field (and in the social sciences generally) are inclined to be materialists – that is, to assume that economics and material interests are primary in determining how the world works. They tend to see political or cultural forces as dependent on economic ones or, at best, lesser-order causes. Sewell questions that assumption, which the example of the dockworkers shows to be unwarranted. Sewell is clearly moving labour history in a post-materialist direction.

* * *

Before the early 1960s, labour history was dominated by a monolithic model of capitalist development. The rise of capitalism meant the growth of the factory system of production, and the growth of factories meant the expansion of a proletariat and therefore the development of radical and class-conscious labour movements. In spite of research that chipped away at the edges of this monolith, it was only with the publication of E. P. Thompson's *The Making of the English Working Class* in 1963 that it began to crumble. Since then, new research has made capitalist development seem more and more multiform. Charles Sabel and Jonathan Zeitlin have even suggested that the factory itself was a contingent rather than a necessary product of industrial capitalism, and that alternatives to mass production may yet win the day against the classic satanic mill.[1] Across the entire range of industries, nineteenth-century capitalist development turns out to have been a most untidy affair.

The history of Marseille's dockworkers in the nineteenth century illustrates with particular clarity how uneven development could create, and in time destroy, a special category of workers. From 1815 to the 1850s, booming maritime capitalism, combined with unchanging technical and organizational conditions on the docks, raised the dockworkers from obscurity to a privileged position unique not only in Marseille but possibly in all of France. Then, in the course of a few years, a capitalist reorganization of dockwork destroyed the dockworkers' niche, reducing them to little more than unskilled labourers. Although the position of Marseille's dockworkers was unusual, their story traced out a broad pattern that has been repeated over and over during the history of capitalism.

The case of Marseille's dockworkers can also contribute to the growing recognition in contemporary historical studies of the autonomy of politics. The classic conception of capitalism as the advance of the factory was always linked to a reductionist

149

notion of the relation between economics and politics. It therefore makes sense that recognition of uneven development should be paralleled by a recognition of the autonomy (or relative autonomy) of politics. Yet the vast literature on artisans, in which the complexity and unevenness of nineteenth-century capitalism was initially documented, has been dominated by a thoroughly reductionist explanatory strategy, an effort to explain workers' politics by their economic experiences.

If artisans were radical, this line of argument goes, it was because their trades, no less than the factory trades, were being penetrated and proletarianized by capitalism, albeit in a subtler fashion. Such case studies as Christopher Johnson's illuminating and seminal article on French tailors in the first half of the nineteenth century have shown that the piecemeal proletarianization undergone by artisans could be economically devastating and have powerfully radicalizing consequences.[2] Moreover, varying forms of capitalist penetration – increasing division of labour, substitution of unskilled for skilled workers in certain phases of the production process, the development of urban putting-out networks or sweatshops, exploitative forms of subcontracting and so on – have by now been documented for a wide variety of trades.[3] This widespread advance of capitalist penetration into the artisan trades in the nineteenth century seems to parallel the widespread advance of artisan radicalism.

But, if capitalist penetration was widespread, it was certainly not universal, nor was it uniform in its effects on the working population. For such penetration to serve as a sufficient explanation of artisan radicalization, it must be shown that radical artisans were drawn disproportionately from those specific trades being degraded by capitalist penetration. As far as I know, this has not been demonstrated. Indeed, the contrary can be shown for the case of Marseille in 1848, where politically radical workers were drawn not only from degraded trades but also from trades that had not been much affected by capitalist penetration and even from trades that had been privileged by capitalist development.[4] The highly uneven effects of capitalist development in the nineteenth century probably created no path of working-class economic experience sufficiently general to account adequately for the broad artisan revolts that occurred.

If this is true, explaining working-class radicalism will require a close attention to the autonomous dynamics of political change itself. Besides asking what socio-economic experiences predisposed workers to radical politics, historians must also ask what sorts of political processes, events and ideologies induced workers to participate in radical political movements.[5] Once again, Marseille's dockworkers serve as an illuminating case, perhaps as a sort of counter-example to Christopher Johnson's tailors. Whereas Johnson's tailors epitomize artisans driven to revolutionary politics by a tragic degradation of their trade, Marseille's dockworkers represent a trade attracted to revolutionary politics in spite of their extraordinary privilege and prosperity. Their history indicates that political processes may produce a broad-based radical working-class movement even when the unevenness of capitalist development fails to produce an economically homogeneous proletariat.

Perhaps the most obvious indication of the dockworkers' privileged position at mid-century was their wage level. Estimates of dockworkers' earnings dating from the 1840s range from 4 to 5½ francs a day. Even taking unemployment into account, dockworkers were among the best-paid workers in the city. Their earnings were at least twice those of other men engaged in heavy manual labour (for example, ditch-diggers or masons' labourers) and were well above those of most artisans, who usually received between 3 and 3½ francs a day. In fact, dockworkers' wages were matched only by such highly skilled workers as glass-blowers, shipwrights, machinists, watchmakers and printers.[6] These high wages were maintained in part by strict limitations on entry into dockworking. It was very difficult to become a dockworker unless one's father already practised the trade. Among dockworkers who were married in 1846 or 1851, no fewer than 70 per cent were dockworkers' sons. This was by far the highest rate of inheritance of any occupation in the city, working class or bourgeois; the next five occupations were fishermen with 58 per cent, rope-makers with 47, tile-makers with 46, tanners with 43 and wholesale merchants (the top bourgeois occupation) with 42. The average rate for all occupations was only 23 per cent.[7]

These figures make it clear that the dockworkers' lucrative trade was a kind of hereditary possession for their families.

The dockworkers' high earnings and high level of occupational inheritance would have been impossible without a powerful labour organization. The dockworkers were organized openly and unabashedly. Their 'Society of Saint Peter and Saint Paul and of Our Lady of Mercy' was authorized by local officials in 1817, shortly after the defeat of Napoleon and the restoration of the Bourbon monarchy. Officially a mutual benefit society, it was actually a reconstitution of the dockworkers' corporation, or guild, from the Old Regime.[a] The corporation dated back at least to the end of the fourteenth century, but its statutes were first written down in 1704. These had been amended in 1789, just before the French Revolution; the statutes of 1814, in turn, were an amended version of those of 1789.[8] In 1814, members of the old corporation and their sons could join the mutual aid society by paying a nominal fee of 8 francs, while all other applicants had to pay 80 francs, a sum equivalent to more than a month's wages for most manual workers. These entry fees were the same as in the Old Regime corporation.[9] In 1841, when the society's statutes were revised again, the entry fee charged for non-dockworkers' sons was increased to the impossible sum of 1,000 francs.[10] Besides erecting these high financial barriers to admission, the dockworkers' society could simply refuse membership to men who attempted to enter, even if they could pay the fee.

If the expansion of commerce posed no immediate challenge to the customary organization of dock work in Marseille, it soon began to strain the physical capacity of the old port. The port was already overcrowded by the 1820s, and by the middle 1830s the situation became critical. Several stop-gap measures were undertaken, such as the razing of buildings along the northern edge of the port to expand the surface of the docks and dredging the port's south-eastern corner to make room for another twenty to thirty ships. But, even after improvements, the docks measured only 3,200 metres for an annual traffic of 7,000–8,000 ships in the late 1840s. It was clear that a new basin comparable in size to the old port was needed. Given the geography of Marseille, this meant a gigantic programme of construction. The new port was fully completed in 1853. As early as 1848, however, the local director of the government's civil engineering corps (*Ponts et chaussées*) had decided that a further northward extension was necessary.[11] The Revolution of 1848, and the financial insolvency and reduction in port traffic that it brought in its wake, interrupted plans for extension. By 1852, maritime commerce began to grow at its pre–1848 pace once again, and the expansion continued through the 1850s and 1860s. By 1856, work began on a series of three new port basins stretching northward along the coast.

The basin completed in 1853 had no significant effect on the organization of dock work. The system that had been used in the old port was simply transferred to the new. But the basins begun in 1856 were a very different matter. The concession for building, equipping and running these basins was awarded to a joint-stock company called the Compagnie des Docks et Entrepôts de Marseille.[b] This company, which was financed by Parisian capital, revolutionized methods of handling cargoes.[12] First, the new dock was what was called a *dock à l'anglais*, that is, it introduced labour-saving equipment, of which steam-driven hydraulic cranes and lifts were the most important. Second, the quays were physically set off from the working-class neighbourhoods of the old city. Third, all goods in transshipment were to be concentrated in warehouses in the new basins rather than being scattered through the city. Fourth, and most important of all, dockworkers were no longer to work in teams for the merchants whose goods were being unloaded: they had to become employees of the Compagnie des Docks. Work was to be organized and policed not by the masters and the dockworkers' society but by employees of the company.

The dockworkers quickly recognized that establishment of the new dock would gravely threaten their position. In the summer of 1864, the dock began full-scale operation. Once again, the Compagnie des Docks insisted that anyone engaged in loading and unloading of ships be an employee of the dock, and once again the dockworkers' society responded by refusing to work under the company's conditions. This time, the company was prepared; it simply staffed the docks with unskilled labourers, mostly Italian immigrants, and offered merchants lower rates than the dockworkers' society could match. The dockworkers' struggle ended in victory for the Compagnie des Docks. Most of the society's members eventually went to work for the company, and the society, stripped of its monopoly, faded into an ordinary mutual aid society that administered sickness and retirement benefits.

The uneven capitalist development that had fortified the dockworkers' privileged niche in the first half of the nineteenth century destroyed it in the 1860s. The general development of French, European and world capitalism caused a massive expansion in Marseille's maritime trade in the nineteenth century. For some decades, this advance in capitalist development did not cause a corresponding advance in the methods of dock work. On the contrary, it actually strengthened an archaic form of labour organization on the docks: the dockworkers' society, which was in fact a carry-over from the guild system of the Old Regime. In this case, the unevenness that characterized all capitalist development also gave rise to combined development: the strengthening of archaic forms in symbiosis with an advanced sector. But, in the end, the exigencies of continuing capitalist development, that is, the need for more space in the port, shattered archaic forms and obliterated the temporarily privileged position of the dockworkers. Marseille's dockworkers were a particular case but a case that fits a very general pattern. The intrinsic and inescapable unevenness of capitalist development promiscuously creates privileged niches for labourers who are advantageously placed in a particular phase of development. But it also, no less promiscuously, destroys the same privileged niches it had created in earlier phases.

At first glance, it would seem that the economic vicissitudes of work had a parallel effect on the dockworkers' politics. The role of dockworkers in the three great revolutionary crises of the nineteenth century (1830–4, 1848–41 and 1870–1) appears to correspond admirably to the evolution of their economic circumstances. The dockworkers seem to have been radical, or at least politically restive, in the first crisis, before their rise to the high prosperity of mid-century; to have been notoriously reactionary at mid-century, when their privileges were at their height; and to have been ardent revolutionaries at the time of the Commune, when their society had been crushed and they had been definitively reduced to proletarian status.

On closer observation, this intimate association between economic situation and political behaviour turns out to be seriously flawed. It is true that the dockworkers were staunch conservatives in February of 1848 and exemplary revolutionaries in 1871. But it appears that their shift to the left began during the period of the Second Republic,[c] several years before the demise of their economic fortunes. The evidence for this shift is scattered, incomplete and not entirely conclusive, but it all seems to point towards a general drift to the left, beginning hesitantly in the spring of 1848, accelerating in 1849 and sustained up to and beyond Louis Napoleon's *coup d'état* in 1851. The first sign of such a drift occurred in June 1848, when radical workers in Marseille revolted at the time of the far more famous Parisian June Days. The dockworkers' national guard company – originally formed as a bastion of reaction – refused to respond to orders on discovering that they might be asked to fire on fellow workers.[13] A year later, there was a sign that the dockworkers were moving towards a more insurgent position. In June 1849, some 500 dockworkers held a banquet in honour of Louis Astouin, a dockworker who had written a widely acclaimed book of poetry and who had just been defeated in a bid for re-election to the National Assembly on the democratic ticket. The banquet ended with the entire crowd shouting 'Vive la République démocratique et sociale!'[d] and some 114 francs were collected for the families of the insurrectionaries of the prior June who remained in custody.[14] Neither of these actions would have been thinkable in the early days of the Second Republic.

All the evidence points to a significant radicalization of dockworkers' political opinions and behaviour between 1848 and the mid-1850s, a decade before the drastic restructuring of work reduced the dockworkers to proletarians. It therefore appears that changes in dockworker politics cannot be explained as a simple reflex of proletarianization. Instead, the seemingly paradoxical rise of dockworker radicalism over the decade following the Revolution of 1848 requires a complex explanation, one that recognizes the simultaneous autonomy and interrelationship of economic, political and social factors.

Let us begin with economics. Although the dockworkers'

favourable structural position in the maritime economy was not challenged in the late 1840s and 1850s, their economic well-being was sharply affected by short-term fluctuations. The traffic of Marseille's port fell precipitously in 1848 and remained low for several years. The revolutionary upheavals of 1848 in France and Europe caused a general panic among the possessing classes; credit dried up and investment fell, causing a depression in industry and trade. It was not until 1852, after Louis Napoleon's *coup d'état* had ended the fear of political instability, that the traffic of the port rebounded to the level of the middle 1840s.[15] The long commercial depression surely increased unemployment and sharply cut incomes on the docks, reducing the dockworkers to economic circumstances more or less comparable to those of the early 1830s, when, as we have seen, they were also involved in revolutionary agitation. The dockworkers were not thrown into desperate poverty by the depression, and the Muse operated to distribute available employment equitably. Indeed, the Muse probably made the impact of the depression less severe for the dockworkers than for most of the city's workers. Nevertheless, lower incomes and high levels of unemployment must have made dockworkers far more receptive to the republican and socialist agitation of the era than would have been the case had employment remained high. This economically induced receptivity undoubtedly helps to explain the dockworkers' initial drift to the left from 1848 to 1851.

These economic changes were paralleled by (and in part caused by) autonomous shifts in the French political system. Most recent literature on the autonomy, or relative autonomy, of politics has focused on the autonomy of the state. States, this literature argues, have their own interests, structures and developmental tendencies that cannot be reduced to the interests of the dominant class, classes or groups. Explaining historical change therefore requires attention not only to the changing conditions of the classes and class fractions that make up a society but also to the changing form and functioning of states.[16] The importance of changes in political structure is clear in revolutionary upheavals. The Revolution of 1848 drastically altered the structure of the French state. The sudden victory of the February 1848 insurrection overthrew a monarch, dissolved a legislative body and threw existing state institutions

into disarray. It created a new but insecure provisional government, which instituted universal male suffrage and abolished
censorship and restrictions on the formation of political associations and trade unions. Under pressure from Parisian
workers, it also declared a new fundamental right, the right
to work, and established the Luxembourg Commission,
headed by socialist Louis Blanc, which was to prepare a new
'organization of labour' for the country. The new and rather
chaotic structure of the French state in the immediate aftermath
of the February Revolution enormously expanded the possibilities for political action by workers. Granted the vote,
allowed to organize in political clubs and trade associations
and promised a fundamental reorganization of the economy,
workers in cities throughout France responded with a frenetic
burst of political activity. A fundamental cause of the radicalization of French workers in general, this change in the structure
of the state must have affected Marseille's dockworkers.

The February Revolution also brought about another closely
related kind of change in the nature of politics that is seldom
considered by those who argue for the autonomy of the state:
a transformation of political discourse. If the hard economic
times of the Second Republic made dockworkers more receptive to messages critical of the status quo, revolutionary politics
changed the character and increased the volume of such messages.[17] The Revolution of 1848 made 'worker' (*ouvrier* or *travaill-
eur*) a politically potent term and made the fact that one
belonged to the socio-economic category of manual workers
politically relevant in a way it had not been before. In Marseille,
as elsewhere in France in the spring of 1848, not only socialists
but public officials, moderates and even the most reactionary
monarchists addressed a blizzard of pamphlets, newspaper
articles, speeches, handbills and proclamations 'to the
workers'. In Louis Althusser's terminology one could say that
after February 1848, the utterance 'worker' insistently inter-
polated or hailed workers as ideologically defined political subjects.[18] Bombarded by this outpouring of ideological discourse,
even the dockworkers, who had been monarchists or apolitical
before 1848, surely were aware that the revolution was promis-
ing to raise manual labour to a new dignity in the state and
must have pondered what their unquestioned status as
workers implied for their own role in politics.

From the very beginning of the revolution, Marseille's conservatives, by ostentatiously adopting the dockworkers as the apotheosis of the apolitical *sage ouvrier*,ᵉ unwittingly contributed to their politicization. Once dockworkers had been encouraged to think of themselves as somehow exemplary of workers in general, they could not be prevented from recognizing that republicans and socialists were hailing all workers as constituents of a new and better state and society, a 'democratic and social republic' in which labour would be properly 'organized' and duly rewarded as the basis of all wealth. By June 1848, the republicans and socialists had not succeeded in constituting dockworkers as revolutionaries. But the fact that the dockworkers' unit of the national guard refused to report for duty at the time of the June insurrection because they were unwilling to fire on 'fellow workers' indicates that they had begun to accept 'worker' as a political identity and to act on that identity even against an express command of the forces of 'order and legality'.

Explaining the changing politics of dockworkers requires that we recognize the autonomy of politics in another sense: that in addition to considering changes in state structures and political discourses, we must also consider the unique details of their political history. From 1849 to 1851, the political history of the dockworkers was closely tied to the surprising career of Louis Astouin, the dockworker poet–politician. Astouin was initially named to the monarchist slate of candidates in the legislative elections of April 1848. The monarchists chose him because of his prominence and popularity as a worker–poet, assuming that his apparent lack of pronounced political views indicated the docile conservatism for which his fellow dockworkers were famous. But in the National Assembly he turned out to be a sincere, if moderate, republican. He was therefore dropped from the monarchist list for the elections of 1849 and replaced by another dockworker of known reactionary opinions. The democrats, however, named Astouin to their list, and he responded by moving considerably to the left and espousing the cause of social democracy. Astouin became a tireless campaigner. Although narrowly defeated in the 1849 election, he continued to work for the democratic and social republic, until Louis Napoleon's *coup d'état* in December 1851. Astouin's towering prestige among the dockworkers, together with his diligent and incessant proselytizing, was surely a major source of the new political insurgency that characterized the dock-workers after 1849.[19]

Three major factors, then, must be taken into account to explain the radicalization of Marseille's dockworkers in the years following 1848. First, the change was made possible by a revolutionary transformation of the state and a consequent upsurge in radical discourse that established 'the worker' as a constituent of a new 'democratic and social republic'. This new vision of work and politics so dominated the discourse of the spring of 1848 that even conservative workers such as the dockworkers could not escape a new politicized working-class identity. Second, the extended maritime depression of the Second Republic doubtless made dockworkers more receptive to the radical message than they would have been in a period of full employment. Finally, the particular political career of Louis Astouin meant that the gospel of the 'democratic and social republic' reached the dockworkers with special authority and intensity between 1849 and 1851. The confluence of these general and particular conditions had the effect of transforming dockworkers from notorious reactionaries to active republicans by the end of the Second Republic.

The dockworkers' politics was hardly a reflex of their relation to the means of production. Socio-economic conditions were far from irrelevant, but the evolution of dockworker politics cannot be explained without reference both to transformations in state structure and political discourse and to the details of politics and personalities in Marseille. To explain how Marseille's dockworkers were radicalized requires not just an examination of their changing economic circumstances but the construction of a multi-causal narrative that takes into account, weighs and attempts to establish the joint and several explanatory powers of social, economic and political factors.

If capitalist development is uneven in the sense I have been arguing in this essay – that is, if it produces not an increasingly solid and uniform proletarian contingent but a continually changing archipelago of variegated working-class categories – then the appropriate explanatory strategy for labour historians is not to look for evidence of proletarianization behind every surge of working-class political radicalism but to ask how and why workers with widely varying economic trajectories and

159

workplace experiences could successfully be constituted as political insurgents. For some trades, in some historical instances, for example, Christopher Johnson's French tailors in the 1830s and 1840s, proletarianization surely is the most important single answer. But we would be wrong to think that the tailors epitomized nineteenth-century working-class experience. This study of Marseille's dockworkers indicates that even highly privileged workers could, under certain conditions, be induced to identify themselves with less fortunate workers and struggle for a radical transformation of the social order. If historians are to understand those occasions when a wide variety of workers joined radical revolts, such as the French workers' insurgencies of 1833–84, 1848–51 and 1870–1, the English Chartist movement, the New York labour uprising of 1850 or the Russian revolutions of 1905 and 1917, we must ask how economic changes, transformations of state structures and political discourse, new or pre-existing networks of social relations and purposive actions by prominent or strategically placed persons or groups made possible the construction – at least for a time – of a common working-class political identity and programme.

EDITOR'S NOTES

a France before the Revolution of 1789.

b The Docking and Storage Company of Marseille.

c A review of political events is in order. The February Revolution of 1848 made Louis-Philippe flee his throne, and France established the Second Republic. Intensified social tensions soon produced bloody conflict between Parsian workers and the army, known as the June Days of 1848. In December 1848, Louis-Napoleon, nephew of the emperor, was elected president of an increasingly conservative republic. He defied constitutional restraints and persecuted pockets of democratic/socialist support. In December 1851, Louis-Napoleon staged a *coup d'état* and created an authoritarian government, a prelude to his empire. There was widespread resistance to the *coup d'état* in certain parts of France.

d 'Long live the social and democratic Republic!'

e Obedient worker.

NOTES

'Uneven development, the autonomy of politics, and the dockworkers of nineteenth-century Marseille', *American Historical Review*, 95 (June

1988): 604–5, 607–10, 623, 627–8, 630, 632–7. Reprinted with the permission of the author.

1 'Historical alternatives to mass production: politics, markets and technology in nineteenth-century industrialization', *Past and Present*, 108 (August 1985): 133–74.
2 Christopher H. Johnson, 'Economic change and artisan discontent: the tailors history, 1800–48', in Roger Price (ed.), *Revolution and Reaction: 1848 and the Second French Republic* (London, 1975): 87–114.
3 William M. Reddy, *The Rise of Market Culture* (Cambridge, 1984); Royden Harrison (ed.), *Independent Collier* (London, 1978).
4 The artisan trades most severely affected by capitalist penetration in Marseille in the first half of the nineteenth century were the tailors and the shoemakers. Their radicalism was surpassed by that of bakers, house-painters and stone-cutters, whose trades do not seem to have been importantly affected by capitalist penetration, and by machinists, whose scarce and avidly sought-for skills made them among the most privileged workers in the city.
5 The socio-economic experiences that can predispose workers to political radicalism need not be either classical or modified versions of proletarianization. Migration, ethnicity, neighbourhood communities, cultural differences or gender identities may, in a given case, be more important than details of the relation to the means of production.
6 Wage figures are from *Travaux de la société de statistique de Marseille*, 4 (1840): 52–3; 5 (1841): 346–7; and 9 (1844): 72–3; and in Archives nationales, C 947.
7 Figures based on analysis of marriage registers from 1821–2, 1846, 1851; and 1869 Archives de la ville, de Marseille, 201 E. See my *Structure and Mobility: The Men and Women of Marseille, 1820–1870* (Cambridge, 1980).
8 Josette Zanzi, 'Les Portefaix marseillais à la fin de l'ancien régime et sous la Révolution française', Mémoire de maîtrise, Faculté des Lettres d'Aix-en-Province (1969): 4–7; Emile Laurent, *Le Pauperisme et les associations de prévoyance*, 2 vols (Paris, 1865), 2: 458–9.
9 Archives de la ville de Marseille: I 1/35, 1370.
10 Laurent, *Le Pauperisme*, 2: 549–50; Victor Nguyen, 'Les Portefaix marseillais: crise et déclin', *Provence historique*, 12 (1962): 363–97. A thousand francs amounted to an entire year's earnings for a skilled worker.
11 Paul Masson (ed.), *Les Bouches-du-Rhône: Encyclopédie départementale*, 9, *Le Mouvement économique* (Paris, 1922): 446–7.
12 Masson, *Les Bouches-du-Rhone*, 9: 450–2; Louis Girand, 'La Politique des grands travaux à Marseille sous le Second Empire', in Chambre de Commerce de Marseille, *Marseille sous le Second Empire* (Paris, 1961); Nguyen, 'Crise': 79.
13 Prosper Dubosc, *Quatre mois de république à Marseille, 24 février–24 juin* (Marseille, 1848): 48.

14 *La Voix du peuple* (8 June 1849). About one-third of all the dock-workers were present at the banquet.
15 Pierre Guiral, 'Le Cas d'un grand port de commerce: Marseille', in C. F. Labrousse (ed.), *Aspects de la crise et de la dépression de l'économie française au milieu de XIXe siècle, 1846–1851* (La Roche-sur-Yon, 1956): 200–25.
16 See, for example, Peter Evans, Dietrich Rueschemeyer and Theda Skocpol, *Bringing the State Back In* (Cambridge, 1985); and Theda Skocpol, *States and Social Revolution* (Cambridge, 1979).
17 See the exchange on these issues between Sewell and Skocpol in *Journal of Modern History*, 57 (March 1985): 57–96.
18 Louis Althusser, 'Ideology and ideological state apparatuses', in *Lenin and Philosophy, and Other Essays* (London, 1971).
19 Astouin's career can be traced from the spring of 1849 to the autumn of 1851 by items in the police files and by articles in *La Voix du peuple* and its successor, *Le Peuple*.

9

ON LANGUAGE, GENDER
AND WORKING-CLASS
HISTORY

Joan Wallach Scott

Charles Tilly noted that 'social historians have generally adopted a broadly Marxist conclusion: that changing interests rooted in the transformation of production account for major alterations in the collective action of Europe's subordinate classes'. That is precisely the point Sewell wishes to question. Recognizing the 'autonomy' of political and cultural forces may well be the dominant trend of the 1990s in social history. It will force a major rethinking of the way we understand the subject — and of the world in which we live.

Joan Scott is a leading advocate of this sort of revisionism. She offers a more radical assessment than Sewell by bringing two philosophical perspectives to her interpretation of history: post-structuralism and feminist theory. The first is a difficult, arcane subject; we cannot really do justice to its complexities in this context. Let us simply say that post-structuralism posits the importance of shared meanings — 'language' is the term used — as basic for knowing reality. Post-structuralists like Scott reject the conventional belief that what we say and think merely describes, in a mostly straightforward manner, the real world out there. Scott contends that the shared meanings come first; they tell us how to interpret the world about us. Moreover, post-structuralists insist that meanings are shifting and unstable. Changes in meaning are hardly random. They reflect power structures and, in turn, create inequalities in access to power.

To post-structuralism Scott joins feminism. She argues that among the most important ways language gives meaning to the world is by drawing upon masculine and feminine associations. This is because differences between men and women have been taken to be rooted in nature and are, therefore, beyond question. Scott challenges labour historians to ask why it is that 'worker' usually meant male wage-earners (and their particular concerns) rather than female wage-earners.

In the following essay, Scott focuses on the gendering of a basic concept of social history: class. She does so by reviewing a recent, noteworthy book. Scott criticizes the author for assuming that class has a fixed, universal meaning. She shows the need to 'deconstruct' the concept, to see how it came to mean what it did. Her analysis demonstrates just how much 'working class' took on masculine associations, thereby marginalizing women. Scott's analysis opens a new avenue of investigation for labour historians: examining how the category of 'working class' has evolved.

It would be unreasonable to expect readers to grasp the intricacies of post-structuralist analysis from this brief reading. In any case, the more important task is to think about how it matters that a masculine concept of class came to dominate.

Scott's insistence on the interpretative nature of concepts accords well with the revisions we have considered in this volume. New labour historians displaced one paradigm and accepted another. Post-structuralism and feminist theory are among the intellectual currents that will push labour history in new directions.

* * *

This essay is an attempt to address a problem that seems to me increasingly evident and stubbornly resistant to easy solution. That problem is the one faced by feminist historians in their attempts to bring women as a subject and gender as an analytic category into the practice of labour history. If women as subjects have increased in visibility, the questions raised by women's history remain awkwardly connected to the central concerns of the field. And gender has not been seriously considered for what it could provide in the way of a major reconceptualization of labour history. Some feminist historians (myself included) have therefore viewed with cautious optimism their colleagues' increasing interest in theories of language. Those theories (contained in the writings of post-structuralists and cultural anthropologists), and better referred to as epistemological theories,[a] offer a way of thinking about how people construct meaning, about how difference (and therefore sexual difference) operates in the construction of meaning and about how the complexities of contextual usages open the way for changes in meaning.

These theories are potentially of great use for the conceptualization of gender and the reconceptualization of historical practice. And yet, for the most part, they have not been used that way. Instead they have been superficially applied, giving feminist historians some cause for frustration, if not pessimism about the kinds of changes we can expect from labour history. The recent spate of articles by labour historians on 'language' demonstrates my point, for they reduce this important concept to the study of 'words'.[1] Words taken at their face value as literal utterances become one more datum to collect and the notion of how meaning is constructed – as a complex way of interpreting and understanding the world – is lost. With the loss of an understanding of meaning, the importance and usefulness of thinking about labour history in terms of gender also disappears. We are left with separate studies of women and of words and those may add new material, but they will never alone transform the way we think about the history we write.

My purpose in this essay is to argue that there is a connection between the study of 'language' and the study of gender, when both are carefully defined; that certain epistemological theories, by providing historians with a way to analyze how gender figures in the construction of social and political meaning, thereby provide us with a way to recast our understanding of the place of gender in history, of the operations of sexual difference in the 'making' of the working class. By 'language' I mean not simply words in their literal usage but the creation of meaning through differentiation. By gender I mean not simply social roles for women and men but the articulation in specific contexts of social understandings of sexual difference. If meaning is constructed in terms of difference (by distinguishing explicitly or implicitly what something is from what it is not), then sexual difference (which is culturally and historically variable, but which always seems fixed and indisputable because of its reference to natural, physical bodies) is an important way of specifying or establishing meaning. My argument, then, is that if we attend to the ways in which 'language' constructs meaning we will also be in a position to find gender. Especially in western Europe and North America in the nineteenth and twentieth centuries – the places and periods

165

with which I am most familiar and in which most labour historians work – the connections are unavoidable. The connections are unavoidable as well because it was precisely in this period that gender was articulated as a problematic issue.

How then have historians managed to avoid the connections for so long? A look at Gareth Stedman Jones's *Languages of Class*, especially his 'Introduction' and the long essay called 'Rethinking Chartism',[b] may provide something of an answer.[2] I choose Stedman Jones not because his work is bad but because it is so good. It seems to me he provides one of the best and clearest discussions so far of some of the uses of 'language' for labour historians and for that reason he has sparked an excited renewal of thinking in the field. Yet his incomplete apprehension of the theories he draws on limits his work methodologically and conceptually; it would be a pity if this were to become the 'new' approach to labour history for it falls far short of the radical promise post-structuralist theory holds out for us and it would perpetuate the marginal status of feminist inquiry in the field of labour history.

I

The theoretical claim of 'Rethinking Chartism' (one I agree with) is that the backgrounds, interests and structural positions of members of the movement cannot explain its emergence or decline. We get nowhere, Stedman Jones tells us, pursuing lines of enquiry that assume social causation because there is no social reality outside or prior to language. Hence class is not a thing whose existence predetermines or is reflected in class consciousness; rather it is 'constructed and inscribed within a complex rhetoric of metaphorical associations, causal inferences and imaginative constructions' (1983: 102). Class and class consciousness are the same thing – they are political articulations that provide an analysis of, a coherent pattern to impose upon, the events and activities of daily life. Although the rhetoric of class appeals to the objective 'experience' of workers, in fact such experience only exists through its conceptual organization; what counts as experience cannot be established by collecting empirical data but by analysing the terms of definition offered in political discourse (by the state, employers, discrete political movements, etc.). The categories within which empirical data are placed, after all, are not objective entities but ways of perceiving or understanding, of assigning importance or significance to phenomena or events. The origins of class must be sought then not in objective material conditions, nor in the consciousness said to reflect those conditions, but in the language of political struggle. '[I]t was not consciousness (or ideology) that produced politics, but politics that produced consciousness' (1983: 19).

This philosophical assumption led Stedman Jones to redefine the nature of Chartism itself – above all it was a political movement – and to propose a new way of studying it – as a 'language' providing the interpretive definition for experience within which action could be organized. Practically, this meant looking at what people wrote and said, but without assuming that the external reality of class explained their words. Stedman Jones's essay is an attempt to illustrate his method. It is a careful reading of 'terms and propositions' (1983: 21) that uncovers the lineage (in radicalism) of Chartist thought and that reveals a real struggle to define the lines of affiliation and opposition for the movement. Without question it 'restores politics to its proper importance' (1983: 21), but only in the most literal way.

Stedman Jones's essay conflates two different definitions of politics: one labels as politics any contest for power within which identities such as class are created; the other characterizes as politics (or political) those goals of a collective movement aimed at formal participation in government or the state. The first definition is by far the more radical for it contains the nonreferential conception Stedman Jones endorses in his introduction. He cannot put into practice the theory he espouses in his introduction because of the methods he employs to analyze history. First, he reads 'language' only literally, with no sense of how texts are constructed. Second, he slips back to the notion that 'language' reflects a 'reality' external to it, rather than being constitutive of that reality.

By treating meaning as 'language' and reading only literally, Stedman Jones finds Chartism to be a political movement because it was interested in formal political representation as a solution to social problems. The key to Chartism, he says, was its use of radical 'vocabulary', the importation of older words and ideas into an early nineteenth-century context. He spends much of the essay showing that the message of Chartism was similar to that of Owenism,[c] trade unionism and the 'Ricardian socialism'[d] of the period – all understood the state as the ultimate source of oppression. Chartism was a heterogeneous movement, including all the unenfranchised in its notion of class; the content of the message, in other words, was political in a formal and literal sense. This procedure shows class to be a political concept not so much because it was formulated in a particular kind of (discursive) conflict but because it contained or referred to political ideas (the vestiges of English radicalism). These ideas, moreover, were the 'effect of' or a 'response to' 'legislative measures of the Whig government' (1983: 175).[e] Political ideas, then, *reflected* changes in political practice and in the position of those who espoused them. Stedman Jones concludes that the rise and fall of Chartism, cannot be 'related . . . to movements in the economy, divisions in the movement or an immature class consciousness' but rather to 'the changing character and policies of the state – the principal enemy upon whose actions radicals had always found that their credibility depended' (1983: 178).

For Stedman Jones to achieve the radical promise of the theory he espouses, he would have to attend to certain aspects he ignores. These are, first, the notion that 'language' reveals entire systems of meaning or knowledge – not only ideas people have about particular issues but their representations and organizations of life and the world. To say, as Stedman Jones does, that Chartism was not a class movement because it sought participation in government is to miss the opportunity to see a larger politics at work, to see, that is, how an identity of class constructed (and contained) social practice, through which people established, interpreted and acted on their place in relation to others. These relations to others – of subordination or dominance, equality or hierarchy – constituted social organization. The problem comes, in part, from using the word 'language' itself, for it somehow reduces the idea of meaning to instrumental utterances – words people say to one another – rather than conveying the idea of meaning as the patterns and relationships that constitute understanding or a 'cultural system'. Stedman Jones's confusion also stems from his use of 'class' as an objective category of social analysis, instead of as an identity historically and contextually created.

The second related aspect of this theory that Stedman Jones overlooks is the way meaning is constructed through differentiation. He assumes a kind of one-dimensional quality for 'language' – that words have a shared and stable definition in all contexts (a 'vocabulary') through which communication occurs. Yet the theorists by whom he is inspired (he cites Saussure)[f] maintained that words acquired meaning by implicit or explicit contrasts established in specific contexts (or discourses). One cannot read Foucault[g] (another presence – albeit implicit – in Stedman Jones's work) without understanding that meaning is multidimensional, established relationally, directed at more than one auditor, framed in an already existing (discursive) field, establishing new fields at the same time. Positive definitions depend on negatives, indeed imply their existence in order to rule them out. This kind of interdependence has ramifications well beyond literal definitions, for it involves other concepts, other relationships in any particular usage. (Thus, for example, seventeenth-century political theorists made analogies between marriage contracts and social contracts that affected how people understood both; and nineteenth-century socialists depicted capitalist exploitation of workers as prostitution, thereby intertwining economic and sexual spheres.) Meaning is developed relationally and differentially and so constitutes relationships. Thus, to apply this to Stedman Jones's subject, one would expect that the category of the working class rested not only on antithesis (capitalists, aristocrats) but on inclusions (wage-earners, the unrepresented) and exclusions (those who held no property in their labour, women and children). The universal category of class, like the universal category of worker, secured its universality through a series of oppositions. The goal of a reading of Chartism from this perspective, it seems to me, is not to reduce it neatly to a formal political struggle or a particular strategy offered by an organized group but to examine the process through which Chartist politics constructed class identity.

It is in analysing the process of making meaning that gender becomes important. Concepts such as class are created through differentiation. Historically, gender has provided a way of articulating and naturalizing difference. If we look closely at the 'languages of class' of the nineteenth century we find they are built with, in terms of, references to sexual difference. In these references, sexual difference is invoked as a 'natural' phenomenon; as such it enjoys a privileged status, seemingly outside question or criticism. Those who do criticize it (and there were those who did) have a difficult time challenging its authority for they seem to be disputing nature instead of social construction. Gender becomes so implicated in concepts of class that there is no way to analyse one without the other. One cannot analyse politics separately from gender, sexuality, the family. These are not compartments of life but discursively related systems; 'language' makes possible the study of their interrelationships. As Chartists set forth their programme they offered the terms of political collective identity. This identity rested on a set of differentiations – inclusions and exclusions, comparisons and contrasts – that relied on sexual difference for their meaning. Had Stedman Jones attended to the way meaning was constructed he would have seen *how* the particular category of class developed by this group relied on gender. By failing to attend to how meanings rest on differentiation he missed both class and gender in their specific manifestations in Chartism.

II

How might Stedman Jones have 'read' Chartism and better captured the process by which the working class was conceived? My answer can only be partial for I do not have the full texts of the documents he cites, nor (since I do not do research on Chartism) can I claim to command detailed knowledge of the field. Still, it seems worthwhile to suggest with the material he offers what a somewhat different conceptual approach to 'languages of class' might have offered.

The Chartists located themselves squarely within the discourse on natural rights. They did this by pointing out the affinity of their constituents – as propertied citizens – with those already enfranchised. Stedman Jones cites rhetoric that projected a future democratic world still consisting of employers and employees to demonstrate that Chartists were not fully 'class conscious'. This kind of reasoning misses the point, for it focuses on the literal content of words instead of on the way meaning was constructed. Stedman Jones tries to prove that Chartism did not reflect real economic conditions by showing that Chartists were not 'class conscious' and he thereby dismisses the way in which class was indeed understood. The terms of his debate with English Marxists overtake his theoretical premises at this point as Stedman Jones tries to show that Chartists were not the forerunners of contemporary socialists. But he grants too much to his opponents, taking their notion of class as the only possible one and arguing that Chartism was not about class at all, instead of insisting that Chartism's 'class' identity was fundamentally different from what later socialists would label 'class'. If one wants to argue that all categories of identity are politically constructed then it makes sense to relativize and historicize the categories. No theoretical ground is gained by reifying the category of class and using that frozen definition as if it were the only possible one.

Not only was the Chartist language setting out the terms of political coalition, but it worked to establish the similarity or comparability of different social groups. The point was to organize working men to demand entry into the political realm by insisting on a common denominator despite certain differences. That common denominator was property, albeit of different types. Chartists developed one aspect of Lockean theory[h] that associated property with the enjoyment of individual political rights, by claiming that the fruit of one's labour or labour power was itself property.[3] As they did so they acknowledged another similarity to those already represented – the fact that all were men. The Chartist demand for universal manhood suffrage acknowledged (what was already in effect in franchise requirements) that only men concluded and entered the social contract; indeed, the identity Chartists claimed with those already represented was that all were male property-holders.[4]

At the same time, Chartism used references to gender to position itself within debates of the popular movement and differentiated itself from certain of its threads, notably those that were expressive, associational and religious. It did so by casting those utopian movements[i] as 'feminine', itself as 'masculine'. (That the Utopians played with gender quite differently is surely significant in this conflict; they projected a future harmonious world in terms of the complementarity of the sexes or of androgyny, positively valuing both feminine and masculine principles.[5]) This gendered differentiation served not only to clarify Chartism's goals but to underscore its argument about the eligibility of working-men for the vote.

Those who contest the notion that the working class (and sometimes, in this rhetoric, 'the people') was embodied in masculine form usually point to the fact that women participated in and supported the movement. This is undoubtedly true, but it does not contradict the argument. Rather, it confuses masculine/feminine with male/female; the former are a set of symbolic references, the latter physical persons, and though there is a relationship between them, they are not the same. Masculine/feminine serves to define abstract qualities and characteristics through an opposition perceived as natural: strong/weak, public/private, rational/expressive, material/spiritual are some examples of gender coding in western culture since the Enlightenment. There is nothing in such usage to prevent individuals of either sex from accepting these definitions, nor from reinterpreting them to explain their own situations. That women supported a 'masculine' movement was not a contradiction, it was rather an affirmation of Chartism's particular interpretation.[6]

The gendered representation of class that Chartism offered, however, *was* a factor in the ways women participated in that movement and in the ways general programmes and policies addressed them. And it probably contributed in the long run to firming up a concept of class that endured long after Chartism's decline. For one, no matter how much later struggles stressed the need for a reorganization of the economy and a redistribution of wealth, the invocation of universal human rights was carried on within the masculine construction of property and rationalist politics. One result of this was to push alternative conceptions of class such as those offered by utopian socialists to the periphery. Another effect was to render sexual difference itself invisible. Class, after all, was offered as a universal category even though it depended on a masculine construction. As a result, it was almost inevitable that men represented the working class. Women then had two possible representations. They were either a specific example of the general experience of class and then it was unnecessary

172

to single them out for separate treatment; for they were assumed to be included in any discussion of the working class as a whole. Or, women were a troubling exception, asserting particular needs and interests detrimental to class politics, objecting to husbands using household money for union dues, demanding different kinds of strategies in strikes, insisting on continuing religious affiliations in an age of secular socialism. Both representations are evident in the history of labour movements and in the writing of their histories and they help us locate reasons for the invisibility of women in the making of the working class.

The masculine representation of class also affected the labour movement's definition of workers' problems. Since women were not considered to have property in labour, it was difficult to find a solution other than removal of women from the workforce to the competitive crises created for certain male trades by the employment of women at very low wages. It was not lack of imagination or male chauvinism that prevented serious defence of the position of women workers, but a construcon of class that equated productivity and masculinity.

The 'language' of class, as Chartists spoke it, placed women (and children) in auxiliary and dependent positions. If women mounted speakers' platforms, organized consumer boycotts and founded special societies of their own, they did so under the Chartist aegis to demand male suffrage and thus assert property rights that came to them through their husbands' and fathers' labour. Eileen Yeo has characterized the Chartist women's position in these terms:

> In their public addresses Chartist women presented themselves mainly in a multi-faceted family role – as the primary tenders of the family, as contributors to the family wage and as auxiliaries who demanded the vote for their male kinfolk in a bid to help the family as a whole.[7]

This implied that women's welfare was included in men's, that consumer activities and childbearing were women's primary tasks, that however public and political these activities they carried a different status than did men's wage work. The masculine construction of class assumed a (gendered) family division of labour; that it reproduced what were thought by some to be natural arrangements makes it no less significant.

173

Nineteenth-century 'languages of class' were complicated, heterogeneous and variable. They were, none the less, indisputably gendered, resting as they did on explicit appeals to nature and implicit evocations (not consciously intended) of sexual difference. We cannot understand how concepts of class acquired legitimacy and established political movements without examining concepts of gender. We cannot understand working-class sexual divisions of labour without interrogating concepts of class. There is no choice between a focus on class or on gender; each is necessarily incomplete without the other. There is no choice between analyses of gender and of women, unless we want to acknowledge the irrelevance of the history of women for the history of class. The link between gender and class is conceptual; it is a link every bit as material as the link between productive forces and relations of production. To study its history requires attention to 'language' and a willingness to subject the very idea of the working class to historical scrutiny.

EDITOR'S NOTES

a Theories about the nature of human knowledge.
b Chartism is a label of convenience for a complicated and changing set of British working-class protest movements in the 1830s and 1840s. Universal male suffrage was the most consistent goal. Chartism has attracted much scholarly attention; recent interpretations have stressed the economic roots.
c Socialist theories stressed by the manufacturer Robert Owen.
d Socialist notions derived from premises enunciated by the economist David Ricardo.
e The Whig party was aristocratic in social composition but liberal in policy – i.e., supporting the industrial–capitalist society that was emerging.
f A linguist who is often seen as a founder of structuralist philosophy.
g A French philosopher closely associated with post-structuralism.
h Deriving from the thought of John Locke, a seventeenth-century philosopher of 'natural rights'.
i Several sorts of early socialist movements came to be called 'utopian' because they depended on persuasion and co-operation, not class conflict. These movements usually called for moral revolutions and the reorganization of family life. They often sought greater equality between women and men.

174

NOTES

From *Gender and the Politics of History* (New York, 1988): 53–67. Copyright © 1988 Columbia University Press. This is a revised version of an article from *International Labor and Working Class History*, 31 (1987): 1–13. Copyright © 1987 The University of Illinois Press. Reprinted with the permission of the publishers.

1 See the editors' introduction to the special issue of the *Radical History Review* on 'Language, work and ideology' 34 (1986): 3: 'As radicals, we are concerned about the languages of power and inequality: how words express and help to construct dominance and subordination.' The conflation of 'language' and 'words' is exactly the problem that needs to be avoided and that I will address throughout this essay. See also Christine Stansell's critique of this essay in *International Labor and Working Class History*, 31 (1987): 24–9.

2 G. S. Jones, *Languages of Class: Studies in English Working Class History, 1832–1982* (Cambridge, 1983).

3 William Sewell, Jr, has shown a similar logic at work among French labourers in the same period. See his *Work and Revolution in France: The Language of Labor from the Old Regime to 1848* (New York, 1980).

4 The political theorist Carole Pateman argues that what was at stake in liberal theory and in concepts of fraternity was not only property generally but men's (sexual) property in women's bodies. See *The Sexual Contract* (Cambridge, 1988).

5 Barbara Taylor, *Eve and the New Jerusalem: Socialism and Feminism in the Nineteenth Century* (New York, 1983).

6 On women in Chartism, see Dorothy Thompson, 'Women and nineteenth century radical politics: a lost dimension', in Juliet Mitchell and Ann Oakley (eds), *The Rights and Wrongs of Women* (London, 1976): 112–38.

7 Eileen Yeo, 'Some practices and problems of Chartist democracy', in J. Epstein and D. Thompson (eds), *The Chartist Experience: Studies in Working-Class Radicalism and Culture, 1830–60* (London, 1982): 345–80.

SUGGESTIONS FOR FURTHER READING

Berlanstein, Lenard R., *The Working People of Paris, 1871–1914* (Baltimore, Maryland, 1984).

Crew, David, *Town in the Ruhr. A Social History of Bochum, 1860–1914* (New York, 1979).

Geary, Dick, *European Labor Protest, 1848–1939* (London, 1981).

Kaplan, Steven and Koepp, Cynthia (eds), *Work in France. Representations, Meaning, Organization, and Practice* (Ithaca, NY, 1986).

Katznelson, Ira and Zolberg, Aristide (eds), *Working-Class Formation. Nineteenth-Century Patterns in Western Europe and the United States* (Princeton, NJ, 1986).

Levine, David (ed.), *Proletarianization and Family Life* (New York, 1984).

Scott, Joan Wallach, *Gender and the Politics of History* (New York, 1988).

Stearns, Peter, *Lives of Labor. Work in a Maturing Industrial Society* (New York, 1975).